ART2-D2'S

GUIDE TO FOLDING AND DOODLING

TOM ANGLEBERGER

AMULET BOOKS
NEW YORK

ISBN for this edition: 978-1-4197-0994-4

Text copyright © 2013 Tom Angleberger
Book design by Melissa J. Arnst

Printed and bound in U.S.A.
10 9 8 7 6 5 4 3 2 1

ABRAMS
THE ART OF BOOKS SINCE 1949

115 West 18th Street
New York, NY 10011
www.abramsbooks.com

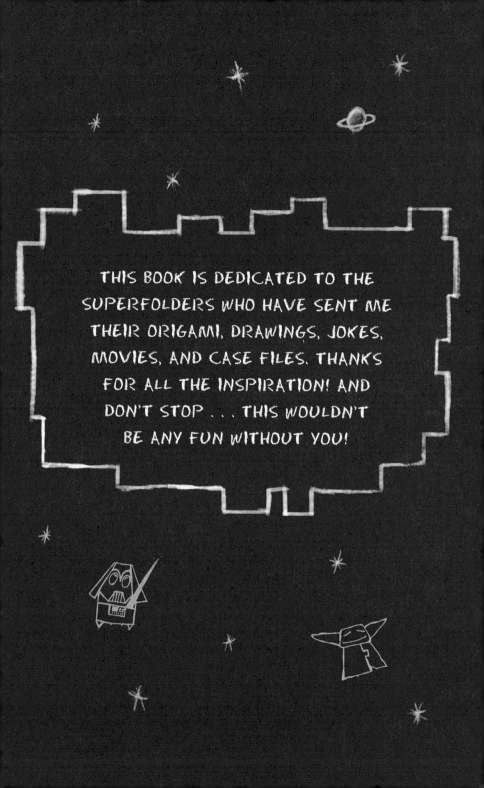

THIS BOOK IS DEDICATED TO THE
SUPERFOLDERS WHO HAVE SENT ME
THEIR ORIGAMI, DRAWINGS, JOKES,
MOVIES, AND CASE FILES. THANKS
FOR ALL THE INSPIRATION! AND
DON'T STOP . . . THIS WOULDN'T
BE ANY FUN WITHOUT YOU!

CONTENTS

HOW TO DRAW PEOPLE

MORE FUN!

ART2-D2 AND
THE NEW (SORT OF)
CASE FILE

BY TOMMY

Okay, so this case file is going to be really weird.

Well, I guess they've all been really weird, so maybe I should just say that this one is weird in a different way.

It all started when Kellen and Dwight came into the library one morning and asked me to help them make their own case file. Well, actually, Kellen was the one who asked. Dwight was trying to balance a pen on his nose. (His current record is one millisecond.)

"This is a million-dollar idea!" said Kellen. "I'm going to make a how-to case file of all of my secrets for being a master doodler . . ."

"A master doodler?" butted in Harvey. "A master drooler, yes. A master doodler . . . uh, no."

But Kellen kept going. "And Dwight's going to tell how to do origami. And Sara can do her smileys, and Murky makes that awesome Chewbacca stamp with an eraser. And everybody can put in something—even you, Tommy—and when we're done, we'll have this awesome case file full of doodling and folding and stuff, and maybe we can even get it published!"

"Published!?!?!?!" splurted Harvey. "You're not going to get it published. Who would want to buy a whole book full of junk like that?"

Dwight let the pen fall to the floor, and he held out Origami Yoda.

"So certain are you?" said Origami Yoda. "Always with you what cannot be done. This

2

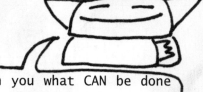

case file . . . teach you what CAN be done it will."

"Sounds awesome," I said. "What should we call it? *Origami Yoda's Guide to Doodling, Folding, and Stuff*?"

"No," said Kellen. "Origami Yoda is going to help some, probably, but here's the star . . ."

And he pulled out this awesome Origami R2-D2. It was folded so that the dome was silver and the body was white.

"It's Art2-D2!" said Kellen.

Harvey's Comment

Somebody hide me until this is done. ←

Tommy's Comment: Aw, c'mon, Harvey. Give it a try. You might even become a *Jedi Doodler.*

Kellen's Comment

MORE LIKE A SITH SCRIBBLER · · · BUT ↙ ENOUGH YAKKING! LET'S GET TO WORK!

BEEP!

BY KELLEN

4

SEE, THERE ARE NO RULES, REQUIREMENTS, GRADES, OR ANYTHING LIKE THAT FOR DOODLING. IF YOU'RE DOING IT . . . THEN YOU'RE DOING IT.

SCRIBBLE IN THIS BOX YOU MUST!

THE ONLY WAY YOU CAN FAIL IS BY <u>NOT</u> SCRIBBLING IN THE BOX. (YOU DID SCRIBBLE IN THE BOX, RIGHT?)

THAT'S DUMB! WHY SHOULD I SCRIBBLE IN THE BOX?

FIRST STEP IT IS IN JOURNEY TO BECOME A JEDI DOODLER.

8

HOW TO DRAW SPEEDY ORIGAMI YODA

BY KELLEN

I'VE HAD TO DRAW ORIGAMI YODA A MILLION TIMES. I FINALLY FIGURED OUT HOW TO DO IT IN ABOUT .8 SECONDS!

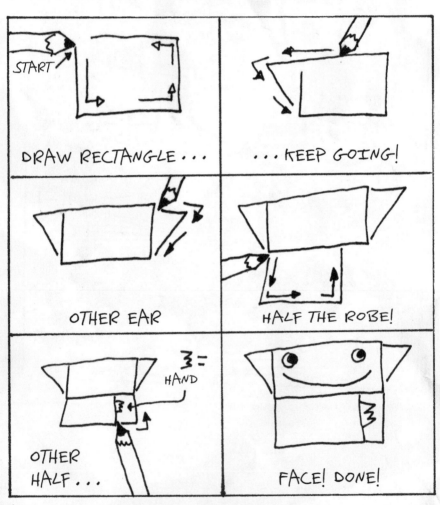

START

DRAW RECTANGLE . . .

. . . KEEP GOING!

OTHER EAR

HALF THE ROBE!

OTHER HALF . . .

HAND

FACE! DONE!

DRAW SOME GOOD ONES...

THEN DRAW SOME FAST ONES!

HOW TO DRAW SPEEDY ORIGAMI VADER

BY KELLEN

DARTH PAPER TAKES MORE LIKE 1.7 SECONDS, BUT HE'S STILL FAST!

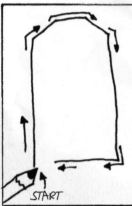

START

...KEEP GOING! MAKE A BIG "M."

ADD EYES... WITH REFLECTION LINES.

RESPIRATOR... WITH LINES

BOTH SIDES OF BODY

DRAW LIGHTSABER AND CONTROL PANEL. DONE!

HINT: DRAW RESPIRATOR LINES TO MAKE A FROWN...   NOT A SMILE!

DRAW VADER...

NOW YOU CAN MAKE THEM FIGHT!

KELLEN

WITH CHEWIE, THE FASTER YOU DRAW HIM, THE MORE WOOKIEE-ISH HE LOOKS!

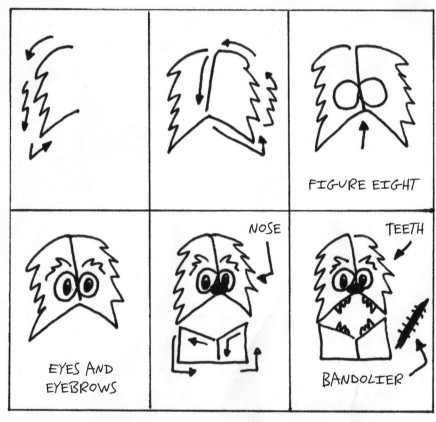

FIGURE EIGHT

EYES AND EYEBROWS

NOSE

TEETH

BANDOLIER

CHEWIE'S BANDOLIER IS JUST A THICK LINE WITH FOUR OR FIVE LINES ACROSS IT. TECHNICALLY, IT SHOULD REALLY BE A THICK BLACK STRIPE WITH TINY WHITE RECTANGLES ON IT, BUT THAT IS A PAIN TO DRAW.

TRY SOME CHEWIES HERE...

HOW TO DRAW SPEEDY ORIGAMI ART2-D2

BY KELLEN

ART2'S BODY IS EASY BUT THE DROID BITS TAKE A LITTLE EXTRA TIME.

FEET

GREAT, NOW I CAN DRAW BAD FASTER!

HOW ABOUT SOME ART2S?

HOW TO DRAW UN-TURKEYS

BY CASSIE

Hi, I'm Cassie! I'm going to teach you how to draw an Imperial AT-AT!

Just turn your hand
outline upside down.
Add some details and . . .

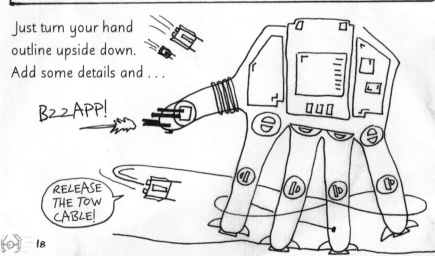

Turn the book sideways
and trace your hand here . . .

What other un-turkeys can you make? How about Modal Nodes?

Try it on this hand, and then try it with your own hand!

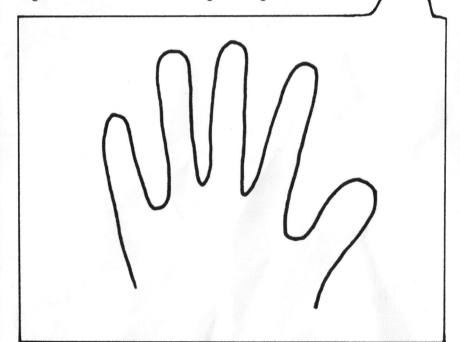

Trace your hand again here . . .

21

HOW TO DRAW
DARTH VADER'S HELMET
BY KELLEN

HOLD YOUR HANDS LIKE THIS. 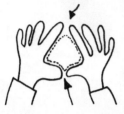 HAVE A PAL TRACE HERE, THEN ADD DETAILS!	ADD HIS RESPIRATOR. 	ADD RESPIRATOR LINES. 
DRAW LADDER. 	DRAW EYE ON EACH SIDE. 	DRAW LINE OVER EYES.  DONE!

YOUR TURN. (TRY NOT TO LET HIS
HELMET GET LUMPY! HE HATES THAT!)

LETTER & NUMBER DOODLES

BY QUAVONDO

 SOMETIMES GETTING STARTED HARDEST PART CAN BE...

BLANK PAGE... FRIGHTENING IT CAN BE.

That's why I like to start with letters and numbers!

Boba Fett		Give it a try...
T + ∩ + 9		
R2-D2		
A + 1 + 1 + E + 8 + 0 + E		
Battle Droid	ROGER, ROGER!	
9 + 0 + E + E + d		

24

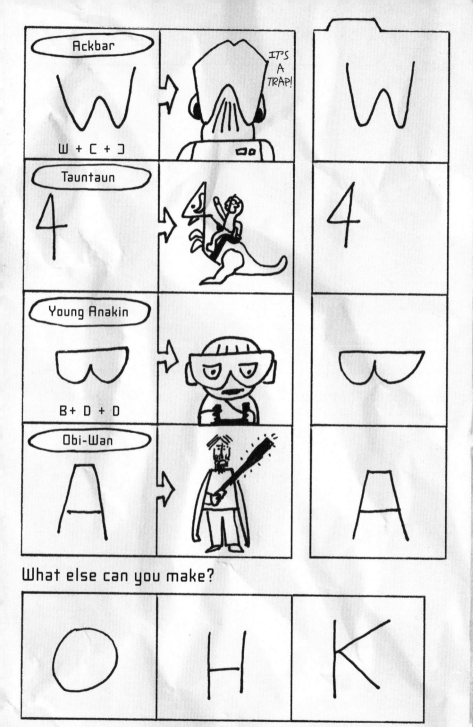

What else can you make?

What can you make with these letters?

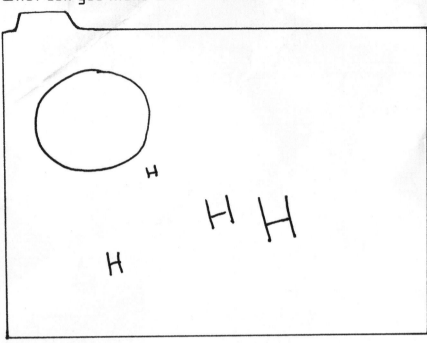

How about this one? Turn it upside down if you want!

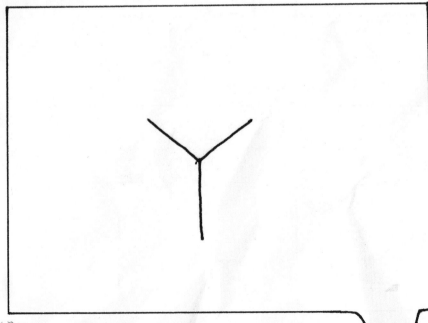

Try your own . . .

STAR WARS
(NOT STOOKY)

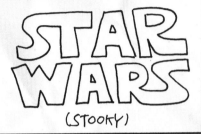
(STOOKY)

CAN YOU IMAGINE IF THE STAR WARS LOGO LOOKED LIKE THE ONE ON THE LEFT???? OF COURSE NOT!! GEORGE LUCAS CARES ABOUT MAKING THINGS LOOK GOOD, SO HE HIRED AN ARTIST TO MAKE THE AWESOMEST, STOOKIEST TITLE EVER...

WELL, I WANTED TO BE ABLE TO MAKE COOL LETTERS LIKE THAT, TOO... THAT'S WHY I CALLED AN EXPERT... THE QUEEN OF <u>BOOK COVER DOODLING</u>...

THANKS, KELLEN!

Okay, first thing to do is to learn to draw around regular letters, like this . . .

Try it . . .

S   W   Q   ?

That was mega easy, right? Well, if you practice a bit, it will get just as easy to draw the outlines without drawing the regular letters first!!!

Just IMAGINE you are drawing around the regular letters, okay?

Note: Try to get the holes in the right places.

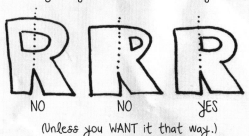

NO   NO   YES

(Unless you WANT it that way.)

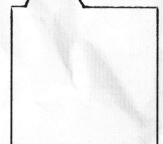

29

3-D letters are easy! Or at least not TOO hard! Let's start super easy with "L" . . .

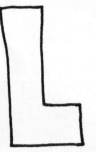

Start with outline.

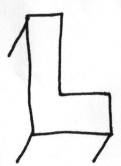

Draw diagonal lines at corners.

Connect the ends of the lines with more lines. And then shade.

Wrong

Right

Don't draw the diagonal lines over the top of your letter. And make sure they all slant the same way.

Wrong

Right

Try with these outlines . . .

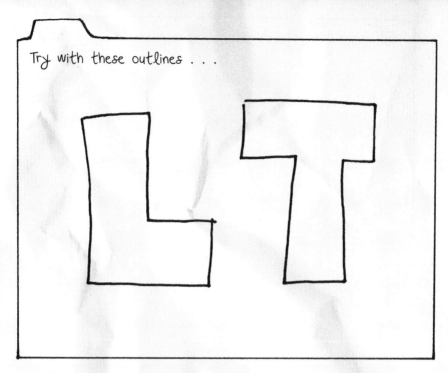

Some letters are harder than others . . . especially round ones! Don't worry about getting them perfect.

Don't forget the hole.

Practice your letters here:

33

TOMMY CAN'T DRAW
BY TOMMY

I'm really hoping this case file helps me learn how to draw, because I stink right now. But I still wanted to be part of the case file! Then I remembered these drawings I saw somewhere.

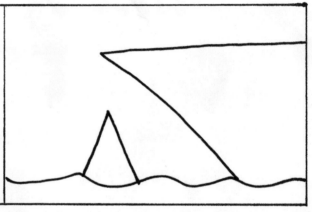

Ship arriving too late to save a drowning witch

You can draw that drawing without knowing how to draw! So I realized it would be easy to change it over to Star Wars . . .

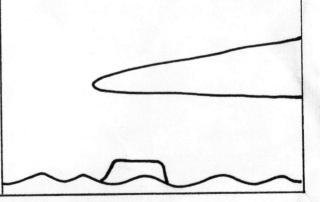

Imperial cruiser arriving too late to save a drowning Cad Bane

See if you can guess what these are:

1.

2.

3.

4.

5.

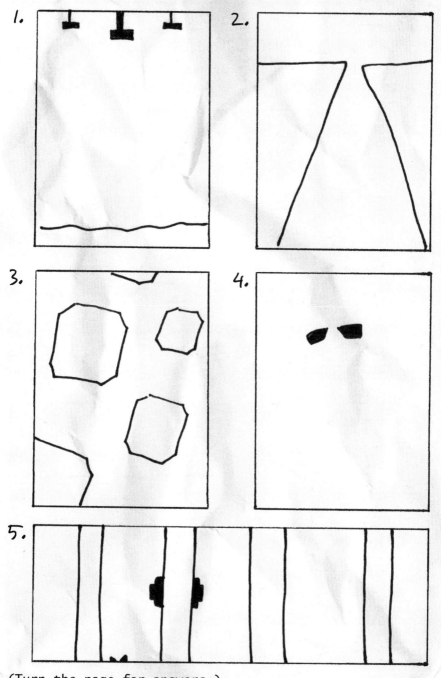

(Turn the page for answers.)

Answers

1. "Put down that X-wing, Yoda!"
2. Too close to a clone, or two sandcrawlers about to bump into each other.
3. TIE fighter attack!! From the side!!
4. Snowtrooper in a snowstorm, or two sandcrawlers about to bump into each other . . . in a sandstorm.
5. Wicket finds Princess Leia hiding in a forest on Endor.

Can you make some?
1. Gonk droid (leg-only view)
2. Close-up of Sy Snootles singing
3. Mace Windu and Ki-Adi-Mundi go for a swim.
4. Close-up of Jabba's tongue.
5. Grievous's cape . . . on a clothesline
6. Make up your own!

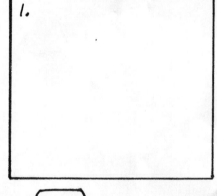

1.

2.

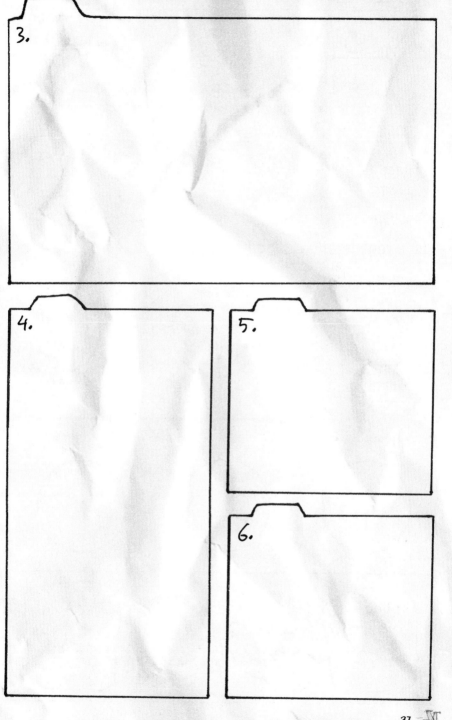

3.

4.

5.

6.

37

SARA'S SMILEY FACTORY

BY SARA

Trace a quarter

Add details

HI! I'M LEIA!

Just a few details will do it!

LUKE

HAN

OBI-WAN

Try here:

( )   ( )   ( )

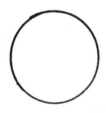

UH, WHY IS EVERYBODY SMILING?

BECAUSE THEY'RE SMILEYS! DUH!

DWIGHT

TOMMY

KELLEN

RHONDELLA

AMY

SNICKERS

MURKY

Your friends here:

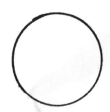 

39

Leaving gaps can be useful . . .

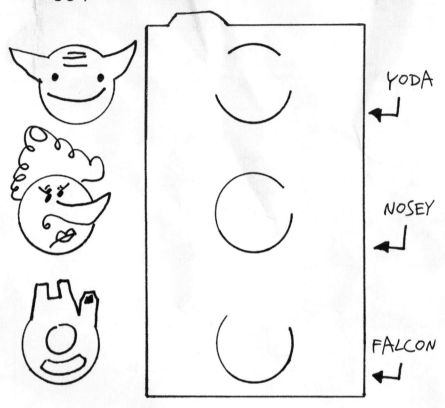

YODA

NOSEY

FALCON

It's all about eye placement!

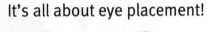

IT'S A TRAP!

Trace top of quarter.

Add a square bottom.

BOBA

BANTHA

JABBA

CANTINA DUDE

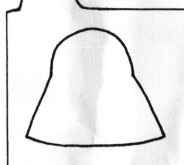

YOU'RE RIGHT, ART2. NOT EVERYONE SHOULD BE A SMILEY!

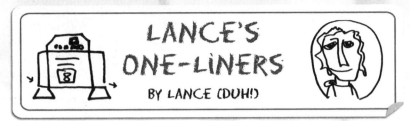

LANCE'S ONE-LINERS
BY LANCE (DUH!)

Don't tell Yoda, but these are almost as easy to draw as stick figures! And they are quicker because you don't lift up your pen (much). Just let it flow!

Here's a Basic Dude:

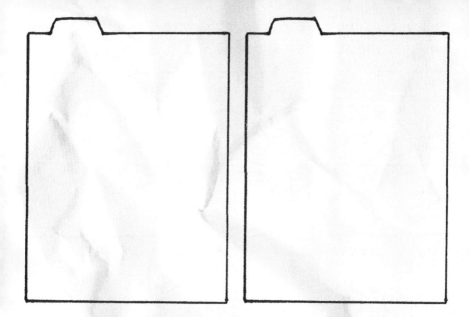

Practice the basic dude a couple times ... then try variations!

Believe it or not, you can draw Jabba with ONE line! (Well, plus two eyes and maybe Bib Fortuna and Salacious Crumb.)

Don't worry, Art2. I didn't forget you!

You can draw most of a dog with a single line. Like this ...

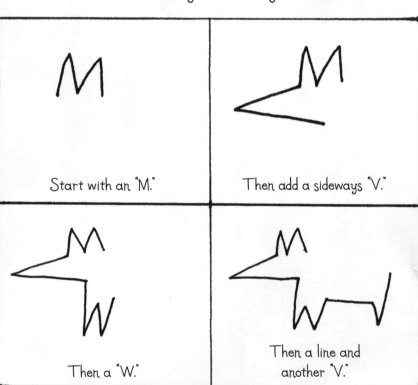

Start with an "M."

Then add a sideways "V."

Then a "W."

Then a line and another "V."

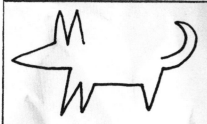

Add any kind of tail you want.

Then draw a line over and up to connect with the ears.

Add dots for the eyes and nose and a thick line for a collar.

Add a mouth and a "V" for the back leg.

Now that you can draw a basic dog, add details to make better dogs!

Space between ears

Google eyes

Spot

Nose

Teeth

Space between legs

Furry

Poo

Different-size legs and paws

You can draw cats the same way!!

UH ... QUESTION: ARE THERE DOGS AND CATS IN STAR WARS?

ANSWER: NO!

FIRST OF ALL, NOT EVERY DOODLE HAS TO BE ABOUT STAR WARS.

SECOND OF ALL, WE CAN USE CAROLINE'S TECHNIQUES TO MAKE FOUR-LEGGED CREATURES THAT <u>ARE</u> IN STAR WARS!

CAROLINE-STYLE STAR WARS CREATURES

BY KELLEN

HERE'S HOW TO USE CAROLINE'S TECHNIQUE TO MAKE THE AWESOME ARENA BEAST, REEK!

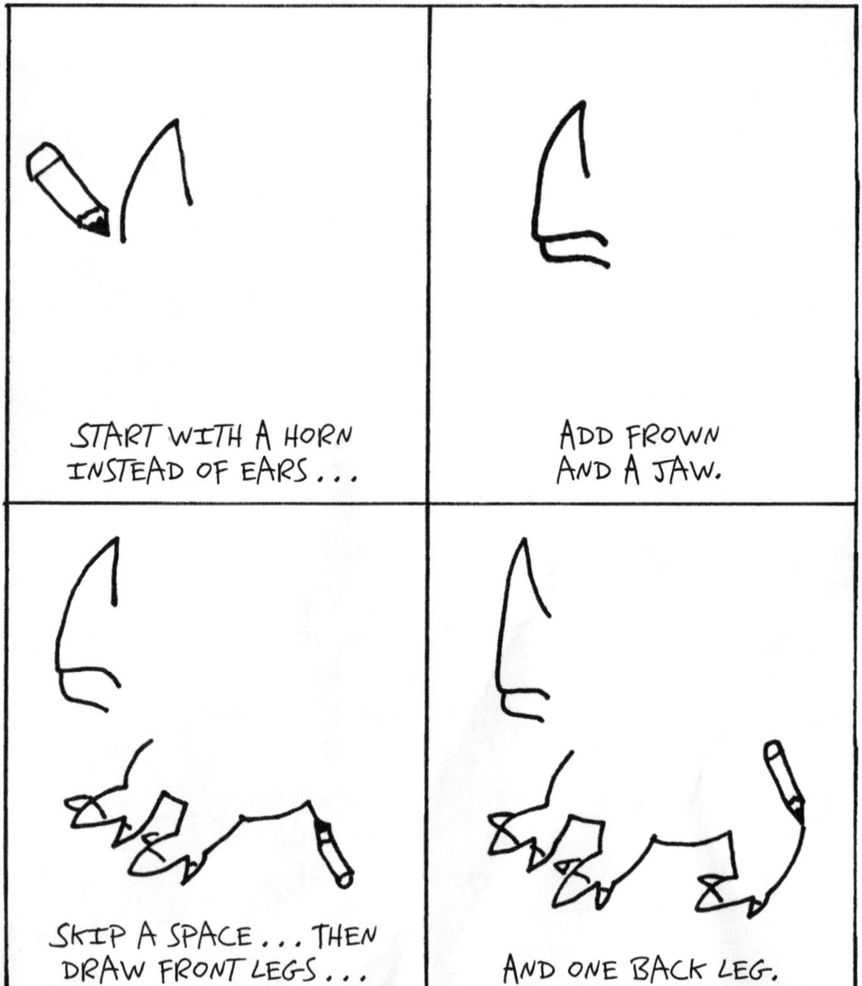

START WITH A HORN INSTEAD OF EARS...

ADD FROWN AND A JAW.

SKIP A SPACE... THEN DRAW FRONT LEGS...

AND ONE BACK LEG.

ADD STUMPY TAIL AND
LUMPY, HUMPY BACK.
CONNECT TO NOSE.

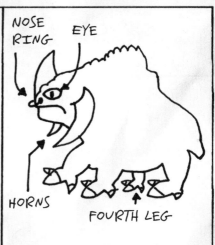

NOSE
RING   EYE

HORNS

FOURTH LEG

FILL IN DETAILS . . .

ADD:
- FOURTH LEG
- DETAILS
- 3-D LETTER EFFECT
- SNOWSPEEDER!

DWARF
SPIDER
DROID

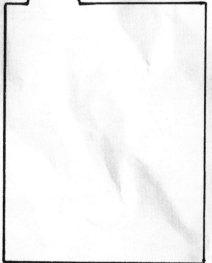

53

DRAW YOUR OWN CREATURES...

SPEECH BALLOONS

BY KELLEN

ONCE YOU START DRAWING CHARACTERS OR CREATURES, YOU'RE GOING TO WANT TO MAKE THEM TALK BY ADDING A SPEECH BALLOON. I DON'T MEAN TO SOUND LIKE HARVEY, BUT... DO IT RIGHT!

BEFORE DRAWING SPEECH BALLOON, WORDS YOU MUST FIRST WRITE!

BEFORE DRAWING SPEECH BALLOON, WORDS YOU MUST FIRST WRITE!

MUST!

BEFORE DRAWING SPEECH BALLOON, WORDS YOU MUST FIRST WRITE!

PROVE IT TO YOURSELF...

WHICH IS EASIER, TRYING TO CRAM ALL THESE WORDS INTO A PRE-DRAWN SPEECH BALLOON...

OR JUST DRAWING A BALLOON AROUND PRE-WRITTEN WORDS?

REMEMBER...

THOUGHTS GO IN BUBBLES, NOT BALLOONS.

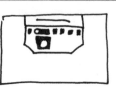

COMPOSITION
BY KELLEN

A LOT OF THE TIME WHEN YOU'RE DOODLING, YOU HAVE TO CRAM IN YOUR DRAWINGS WHEREVER YOU CAN. BUT IF YOU'VE GOT A BUNCH OF SPACE TO FILL, TRY TO DO IT WITH STYLE...

DOODLE-GAMI
BY DWIGHT AND KELLEN

DWIGHT MAKES THE ORIGAMI.

+

KELLEN MAKES THE DOODLES.

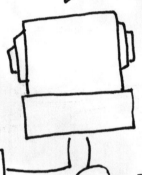

TOGETHER THEY MAKE... DOODLE-GAMI!!!

DOODLE-GAMI? SERIOUSLY?

YES! NOW HUSH UP, CUT A PIECE OF PAPER INTO FOUR PIECES, AND START FOLDING!

FIRST, DWIGHT WILL SHOW US HOW TO MAKE THE
WORLD'S SIMPLEST FINGER PUPPET! JUST THREE FOLDS!

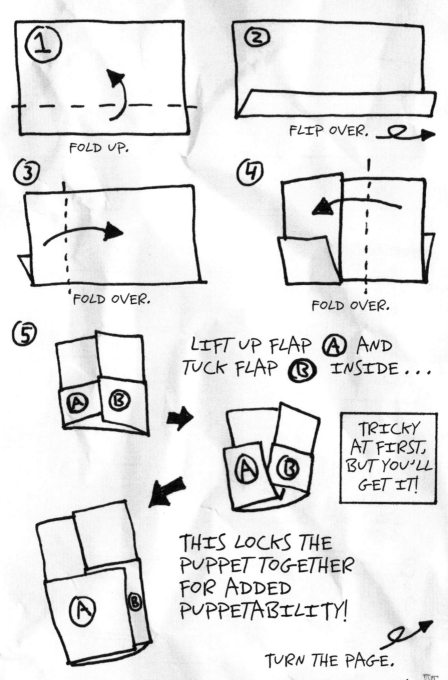

① FOLD UP.

② FLIP OVER.

③ FOLD OVER.

④ FOLD OVER.

⑤ LIFT UP FLAP Ⓐ AND
TUCK FLAP Ⓑ INSIDE...

TRICKY
AT FIRST,
BUT YOU'LL
GET IT!

THIS LOCKS THE
PUPPET TOGETHER
FOR ADDED
PUPPETABILITY!

TURN THE PAGE.

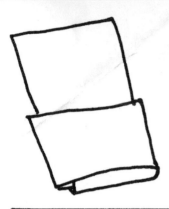

FLIP PUPPET OVER. NOW YOU HAVE A BLANK PUPPET THAT YOU CAN TURN INTO ALMOST ANYBODY BY DOODLING ON IT!

HINT: PRACTICE YOUR DOODLE FIRST, BEFORE YOU DRAW ON THE FINGER PUPPET!

NOW TRY SOME EASY VARIATIONS TO GET DIFFERENT
PUPPETS. START WITH PAPER TALL INSTEAD OF SHORT.

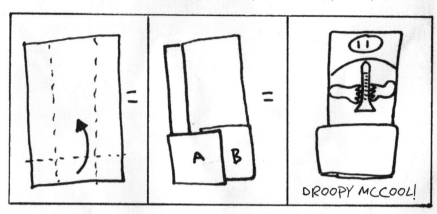

DROOPY McCOOL!

OR TRY MAKING FOLD 1 BIGGER . . .

ROTATE!

MR. HOWELL!

OR BEND CORNERS DOWN TO ROUND HEAD.

RHRR!

HERE'S A HAIRY VARIATION!

BETWEEN STEPS 1 AND 2, ADD A FOLD OR TWO TO CREATE HAIR . . .

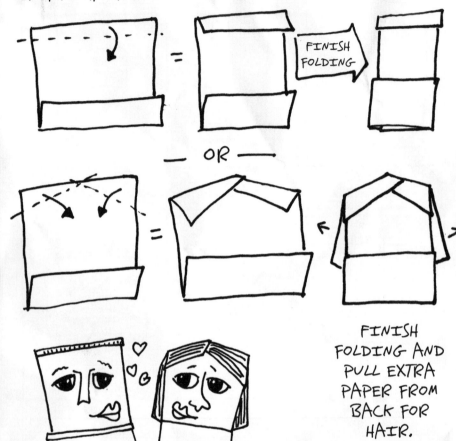

FINISH FOLDING AND PULL EXTRA PAPER FROM BACK FOR HAIR.

AND HERE'S AN IMPERIAL VARIATION!
STORMTROOPERS AND CLONE TROOPERS!

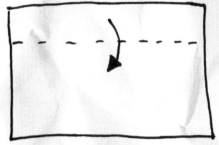

FOLD DOWN.

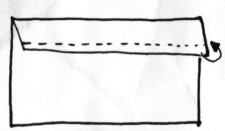

FOLD UP A THIN STRIP.

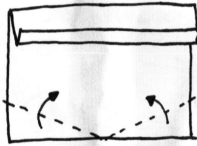

FOLD UP CORNERS.

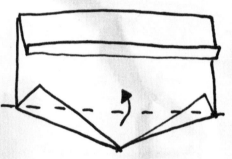

FOLD POINT UP.

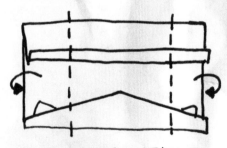

NOW FOLD SIDES BACK
LIKE WITH THE BASIC
PUPPET. (BUT DON'T
TUCK FLAPS YET!)

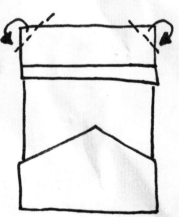

FOLD BACK CORNERS TO
MAKE HELMET ROUND.

65

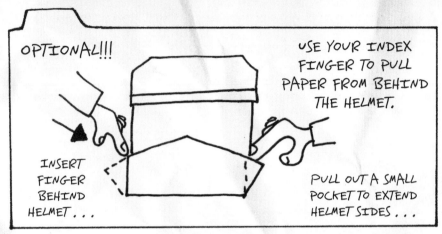

OPTIONAL!!!

USE YOUR INDEX FINGER TO PULL PAPER FROM BEHIND THE HELMET.

INSERT FINGER BEHIND HELMET . . .

PULL OUT A SMALL POCKET TO EXTEND HELMET SIDES . . .

COLOR THIS WHOLE STRIP.

EYES ARE ROUNDED TRIANGLES.

MAKE A TRIANGLE ABOVE FLAP, THEN FILL WITH THICK LINES. (MOVE FLAP TO MAKE DRAWING EASIER.)

DON'T FORGET THIS STUFF.

PHASE II

WITH SOME TWEAKS YOU CAN MAKE CLONES!

REX

BUT MAKE SURE YOU GET THEIR MARKINGS RIGHT!

UNIVERSAL PUPPET
BY DWIGHT AND KELLEN

YOU CAN MAKE THIS PUPPET INTO ALMOST ANYTHING . . . DEPENDING ON HOW YOU START.

TURN YOUR PAPER EITHER . . .

SHORT
(LIKE
ART2-D2)

OR

TALL
(LIKE
C-3PO)

EITHER WAY, THE FOLDS ARE BASICALLY THE SAME . . . LET'S START WITH SHORT!

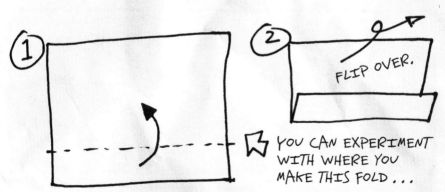

①

② FLIP OVER.

YOU CAN EXPERIMENT WITH WHERE YOU MAKE THIS FOLD . . .

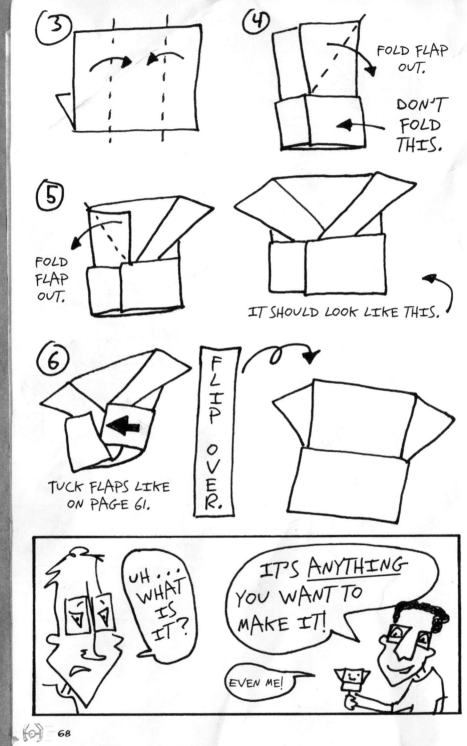

BY MESSING WITH THE EARFLAPS, TWEAKING THE FOLDS, AND DOODLING, YOU CAN MAKE THE UNIVERSAL PUPPET INTO (ALMOST) ANYBODY!

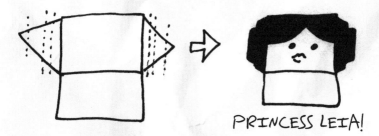

PRINCESS LEIA!

DON'T BE AFRAID TO **EXPERIMENT!**

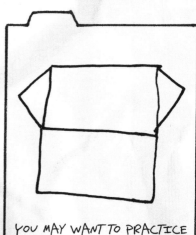

YOU MAY WANT TO PRACTICE YOUR DRAWING FIRST...

ART2-D2
AND C-3PO
BY DWIGHT AND KELLEN

YOU CAN USE THE UNIVERSAL TECHNIQUE
TO MAKE BOTH DROIDS! FIRST: ART2!

①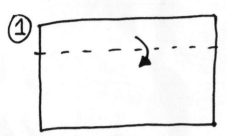

FOLD TOP DOWN.
(NOT TOO FAR!)

②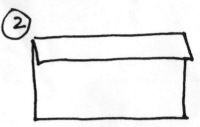

FLIP OVER. ℮

③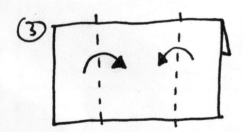

FOLD BOTH SIDES OVER.

④ INSTEAD OF
FOLDING THE TOP
CORNERS OUT,
WE'LL USE THE
BOTTOM CORNERS
HERE . . .

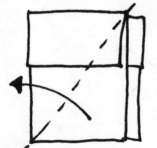

LIKE THIS . . .

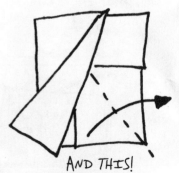

AND THIS!

(NOTE: DOTTED LINE GOES FROM CORNER TO CORNER.)

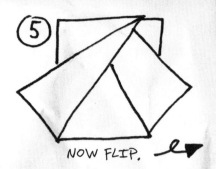

(5) NOW FLIP. ➴➤

(6) LOOKS A LITTLE LIKE ARTZ, RIGHT?

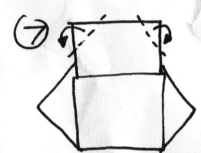

(7) FOLD BACK CORNERS TO MAKE DOME.

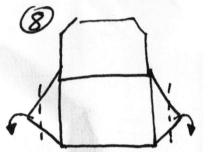

(8) FOLD BACK CORNERS TO FORM LEGS.

(9) FOLD A BIT OF BOTTOM BACK.

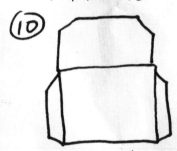

(10) DONE! NOW DECORATE!

SIMPLE OR DETAILED

NOW C-3PO WILL
BE EASY! JUST START
WITH YOUR PAPER
TALL AND THEN FOLLOW
ALL OF THE ART2 STEPS
EXCEPT #9. →

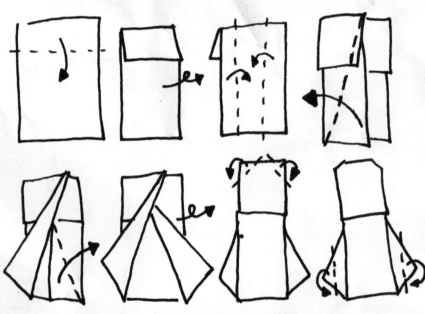

NOW DECORATE!

HINT: EYES ARE
CIRCLE + LINES + A DOT.

ONE MORE FOLD

BY DWIGHT AND KELLEN

① QUICKLY COLOR ONE SIDE BROWN... CRAYON

FLIP.

② AND ONE SIDE GREEN. CRAYON

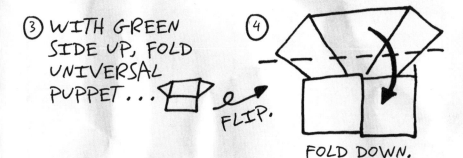

③ WITH GREEN SIDE UP, FOLD UNIVERSAL PUPPET...

FLIP.

④

FOLD DOWN.

DRAW FACE.

TUCK LIGHTSABER HERE. (SEE PAGE 75.)

OR · · · TRY TALL! LEAVE ONE SIDE WHITE.
COVER THE OTHER WITH ORANGE DOTS.

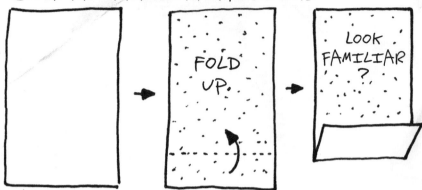

FOLD UP.

LOOK FAMILIAR?

NOW FOLLOW THE REST OF THE UNIVERSAL PUPPET INSTRUCTIONS.

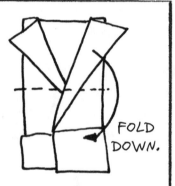

FOLD DOWN.

YOU SHOULD HAVE SOMETHING LIKE THIS . . .

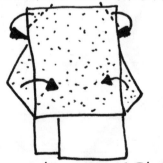

FOLD HEAD CORNERS BACK AND EYE TRIANGLES OVER.

IT'S A TRAP!

ADD EYES, MOUTH, UNIFORM STUFF.

LASTLY . . . LIGHTSABERS!

BY DWIGHT AND KELLEN

CUT PAPER IN HALF.

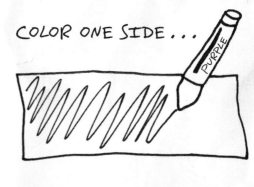

COLOR ONE SIDE . . .

PURPLE

NOW FINISH LIKE A THREE-FOLD PUPPET!

① FOLD UP.

② FOLD BACK.

③ TUCK FLAPS IN BACK.

NICE AND STURDY

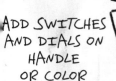

ADD SWITCHES AND DIALS ON HANDLE OR COLOR BLACK.

M.W.

READY FOR ACTION!

DARTH PAPER

INVENTED BY HARVEY
DRAWN BY KELLEN

BEN'S

At last! I, Harvey, will finally reveal how to fold Darth Paper! Not Ben's Darth Paper (which I admit was pretty good) but MY Darth Paper! The REAL Darth Paper! But it's not easy! This is advanced stuff. First make sure you know how to make a pleat ...

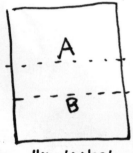

How to pleat

Fold up on A ...

and down on B.

Result: a paper zigzag!

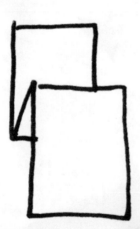

Side view

Okay . . . ready for Darth?

① fold like you're starting an airplane, but . . .

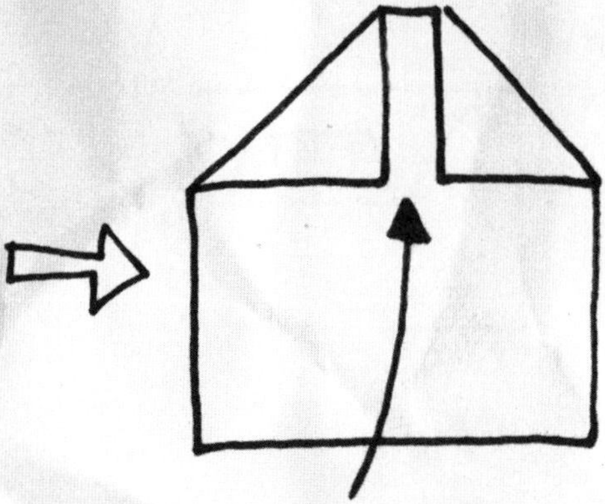

leave a gap!

② fold top down.

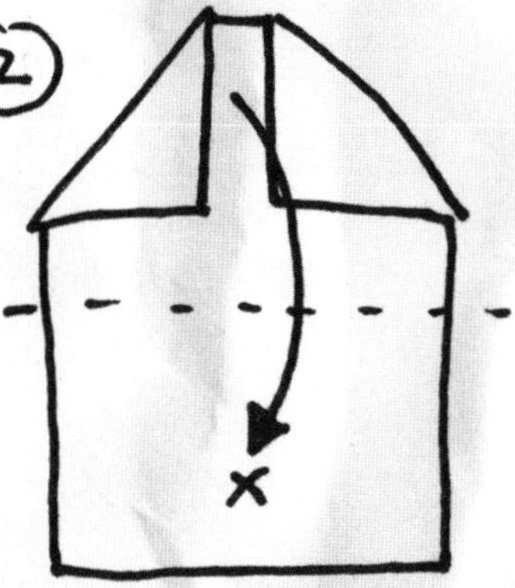

③ fold down again.

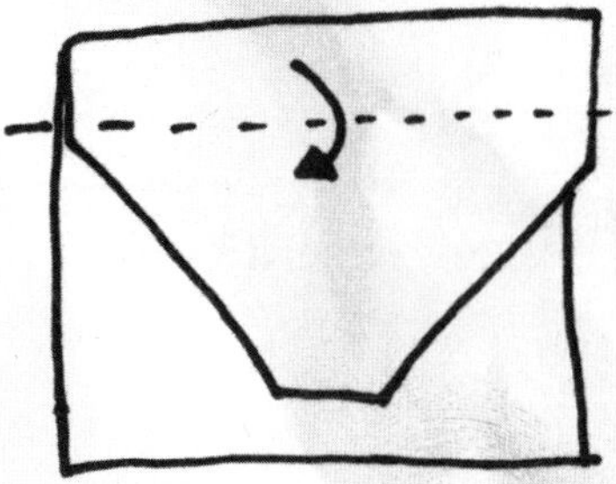

④ fold tip up.

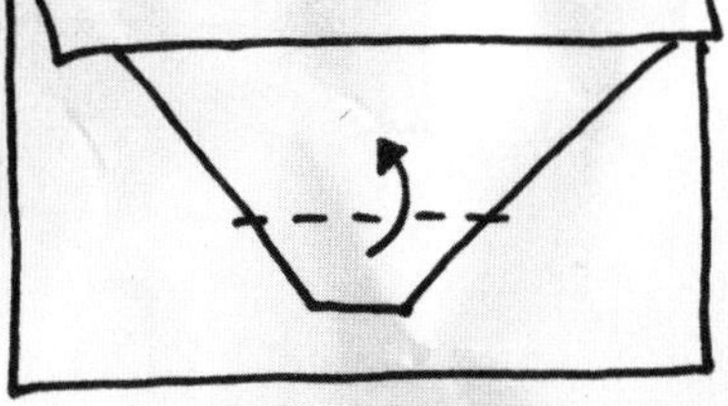

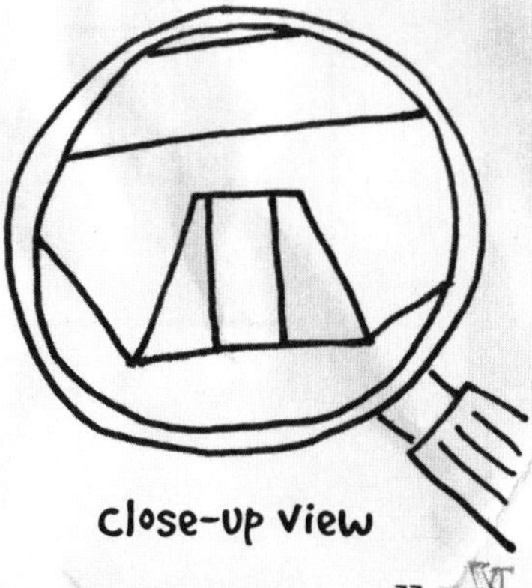

close-up view

77

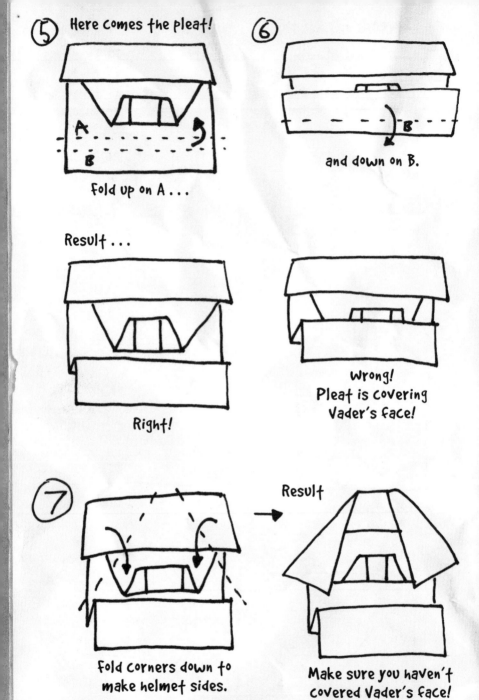

5 Here comes the pleat!

fold up on A ...

6 and down on B.

Result ...

Right!

Wrong!
Pleat is covering
Vader's face!

7 fold corners down to
make helmet sides.

Result

Make sure you haven't
covered Vader's face!
(He hates that!)

⑧ This is a hard fold, because you have to bend many layers of paper!

fold sides BEHIND helmet

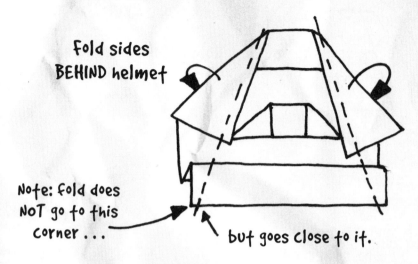

Note: fold does NOT go to this corner ...

but goes close to it.

⑨ Result ...

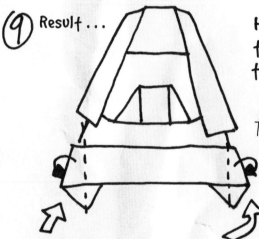

Hopefully, you will get two triangular legs at the bottom. If not, try re-doing step 8.

Tommy's note: Impossible!

Now fold the sides back— being careful NOT to fold helmet again, just the lower sides.

Result ...

10

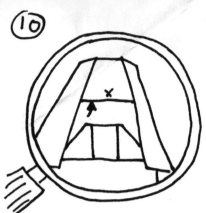

Now make Vader's famous helmet eyebrows.

Hold X with right thumb. Push paper upward with left thumb.

11

Now switch fingers and push up the other side. Be careful not to rip it.

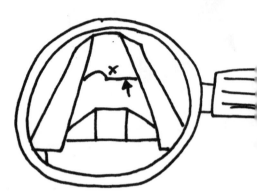

12

Decorate and put a lightsaber in pleat.

To use...

Put finger in pleat. **or** Put finger under mask.

Tommy's comment: Don't get upset if it looks lame the first time. Even Harvey needed practice to get all those gaps and folds in the right places!

Everybody always asks me how to have Anakin's head under the mask ... That's the genius part of MY version of Darth Paper. Anakin's head is already in there!

If you pull up on Darth Paper's mask, you'll think it won't come up. But if you pull on one side at a time ... a hidden PLEAT will pop loose!

Pop both sides loose and you'll find the perfect spot to draw Anakin's face!

NOOOOOO!

ORIGAMI YODA VS. DARTH PAPER
BY KELLEN

YOU CAN MAKE YOUR ORIGAMI PUPPETS FIGHT

KIRIGAMI GENERAL GRIEVOUS

BY DWIGHT AND KELLEN

KIRIGAMI LIKE ORIGAMI IS, BUT THE PAPER CUT WITH SCISSORS IS. OPEN UP MILLIONS OF NEW POSSIBILITIES IT DOES...

LAME!

IF YOU CUT THE PAPER, THEN IT'S NOT REAL ORIGAMI! JUST LAME ORIGAMI!

WHO DARES TO CALL ME LAME?

UH, NOT ME!

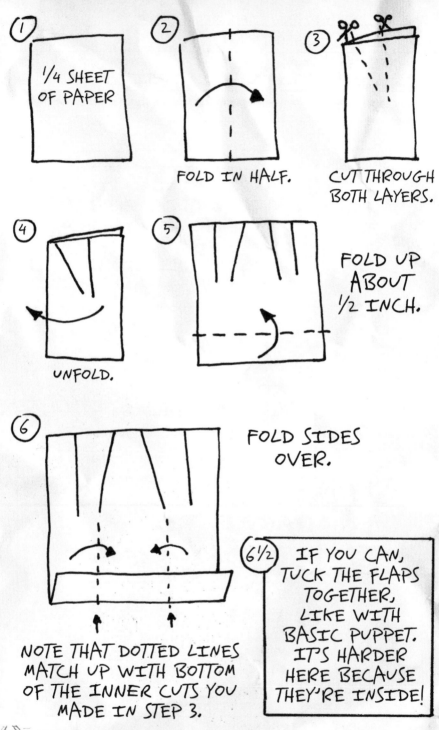

1. 1/4 SHEET OF PAPER

2. FOLD IN HALF.

3. CUT THROUGH BOTH LAYERS.

4. UNFOLD.

5. FOLD UP ABOUT 1/2 INCH.

FOLD SIDES OVER.

6. NOTE THAT DOTTED LINES MATCH UP WITH BOTTOM OF THE INNER CUTS YOU MADE IN STEP 3.

6½. IF YOU CAN, TUCK THE FLAPS TOGETHER, LIKE WITH BASIC PUPPET. IT'S HARDER HERE BECAUSE THEY'RE INSIDE!

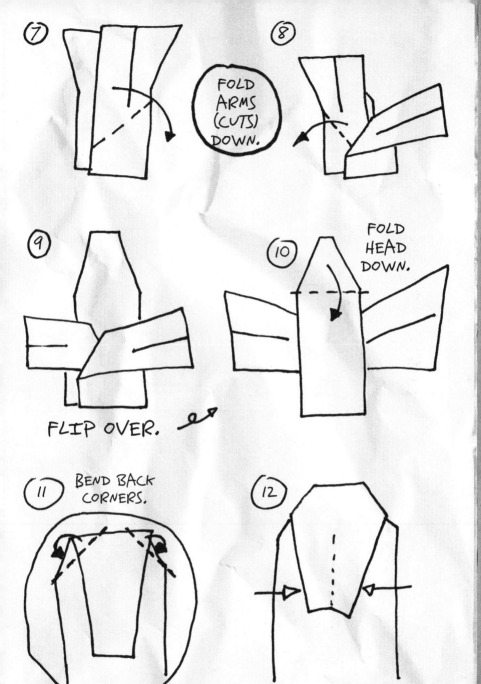

⑦

FOLD ARMS (CUTS) DOWN.

⑧

⑨

FLIP OVER.

⑩

FOLD HEAD DOWN.

⑪ BEND BACK CORNERS.

CLOSE-UP VIEW

⑫

PINCH SIDES OF HEAD GENTLY TO CREATE 3-D EFFECT.

85

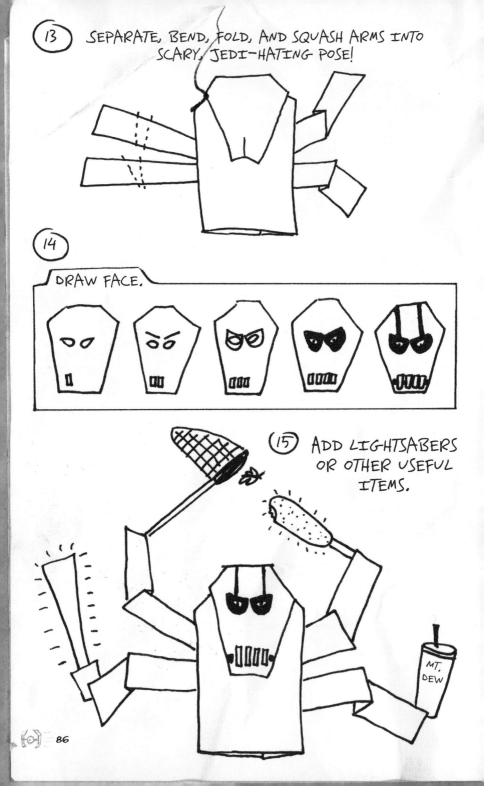

13. SEPARATE, BEND, FOLD, AND SQUASH ARMS INTO SCARY, JEDI-HATING POSE!

14.

DRAW FACE.

15. ADD LIGHTSABERS OR OTHER USEFUL ITEMS.

MT. DEW

ORIGAMI COSTUMES

BY SARA, TOMMY, AND KELLEN

① SEE IF YOU CAN TALK A TEACHER INTO GIVING YOU FOUR OR FIVE FEET OF BULLETIN BOARD PAPER. (THEY'VE PROBABLY GOT GIANT ROLLS OF IT HIDDEN IN THE TEACHERS' LOUNGE OR SOMEWHERE...)

② IF NOT, YOU'LL HAVE TO FIND AN ART, PAPER, PARTY, OR CRAFTS STORE. ONCE YOU FIND THE PAPER, IT'S PRETTY CHEAP.

③ FOLD YOUR ORIGAMI. (YOU'LL WANT TO PRACTICE WITH A SMALL PIECE OF PAPER FIRST, OF COURSE.) FOR THE BIG ONE, USE PLENTY OF TAPE.

④ CHOOSE HOW YOU ARE GOING TO WEAR IT: OVER YOUR HEAD OR WITH A HOLE FOR YOUR HEAD. CUT EYEHOLES... OR ... CUT A HEAD HOLE.

WHITE SLEEVES

NOTE: DON'T CUT THE HOLES WHILE YOU ARE INSIDE!!! MURKY KNEW A KID WHO CUT OFF HIS NOSE THIS WAY AND HAS TO WEAR A FAKE ONE. NO JOKE!!!

87

FOLDING 1,000 YODAS

BY ORIGAMI MASTER BEN AND KELLEN

GET 250 SHEETS OF PAPER...

CUT THEM IN HALF...

CUT THOSE IN HALF...

NOW YOU HAVE 1,000 RECTANGLES!

CHOOSE

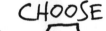

FIVE-FOLD YODAS LIKE IN THE DARTH PAPER CASE FILE... A HUGE TASK

OR REGULAR YODAS FROM THE ORIGAMI YODA CASE FILE... A <u>MONSTER</u> HUGE TASK!!!

EITHER WAY...
MUCH PATIENCE WILL
YOU NEED!

GAIN JEDI WISDOM
YOU WILL?

OR JUST BIG
MESS?

YOU CAN FIND INSTRUCTIONS FOR BOTH YODAS ON
TOMMY'S WEB SITE: ORIGAMIYODA.COM

DON'T WASTE
THE COLOR PAGES
BY KELLEN

<u>PRACTICE</u> ON REGULAR PAPER BEFORE YOU PULL OUT THESE COLOR PAGES TO USE FOR YOUR ORIGAMI!!!!! DO YOU KNOW HOW MUCH IT COST TO HAVE THEM PRINTED? <u>A LOT</u>!!!!!

WHEN WE FOUND OUT HOW MUCH, I HAD TO ASK MY MOM FOR THE EXTRA MONEY. SHE SAID SHE WOULD GIVE IT TO ME IF I WOULD <u>LET</u> HER PUT AN AD IN THE CASE FILE.

SHE SAID IT WOULD BE LIKE A PUBLIC SERVICE MESSAGE. I DIDN'T HAVE A CHOICE, SO HERE IT IS . . .

Kellen,

I am so proud of you and the other kids for putting this book together. Your drawings and projects are really wonderful, and you all have very promising futures . . .

. . . if you can learn how to do things more neatly.

I just can't understand why you would work so hard on something like this and then let it get all crumpled up.

And the handwriting! How can you expect other people to read your comics if you are going to scrawl the words in the speech balloons?

So keep it neat and you'll go far!

Love,
MOM!

Harvey's Comment

How embarrassing . . . especially since she's right!

89

FOLDING THE COLOR PAGES...

DWIGHT SAYS THE HARDEST THING ABOUT ORIGAMI CAN BE FINDING THE COLOR PAPER YOU WANT. HERE WE'VE GIVEN YOU COLOR COMBINATIONS FOR MAKING FIVE COOL STAR WARS CHARACTERS. SO, LIKE I SAID BEFORE, USE THIS PAPER CAREFULLY. FOLD ALONG THE PERFORATED LINE BEFORE YOU TEAR THE PAPER OUT AND MAYBE PRACTICE ON REGULAR PAPER FIRST.

- THE GRAY/ WHITE SHEET IS FOR FOLDING ART2-D2. USE THE INSTRUCTIONS FROM PAGE 70. START WITH THE PAPER WHITE SIDE UP, SO THAT THE FIRST FOLD CREATES A GRAY DOME ON TOP OF A WHITE BODY.

- THE GOLD/GOLD PAPER IS FOR C-3PO. USE THE INSTRUCTIONS FROM PAGE 72.

- THE BROWN/GREEN PAPER IS FOR YODA. USE THE INSTRUCTIONS FROM PAGE 73. START WITH THE GREEN SIDE UP, SO THAT THE FIRST FOLD FORMS HIS BROWN ROBE. OR YOU CAN USE THE INSTRUCTIONS FROM TOMMY'S FIRST CASE FILE, THE STRANGE CASE OF ORIGAMI YODA. TO DO THAT ONE, START WITH THE BROWN SIDE UP. TOMMY HAS ALSO POSTED THOSE INSTRUCTIONS TO HIS WEB SITE, ORIGAMIYODA.COM.

- THE ORANGE/WHITE PAPER IS FOR ADMIRAL ACKBAR. USE THE INSTRUCTIONS FROM PAGE 74. START WITH THE ORANGE SIDE UP, SO THAT THE FIRST FOLD CREATES HIS WHITE UNIFORM.

- THE BLACK/BLACK PAPER IS FOR DARTH PAPER! YOU CAN USE THE (NEARLY IMPOSSIBLE) INSTRUCTIONS FOR HARVEY'S DARTH PAPER ON PAGE 76. OR YOU CAN USE BEN'S MUCH SIMPLER INSTRUCTIONS FROM TOMMY'S SECOND CASE FILE, DARTH PAPER STRIKES BACK, WHICH ARE ALSO ON ORIGAMIYODA.COM.

PHOTOGRAPHING DOODLE-GAMI PUPPETS

BY RHONDELLA

Uh . . . doodle-gami? You're actually calling it doodle-gami?

Only you guys could make *Star Wars* finger puppets MORE embarrassing!

Anyway, the only reason I'm doing this is because you all are always sending me these dark, blurry pictures of stuff. Like this . . .

Seriously? Even before I was on the yearbook staff I could take better pictures than that!

So, I'm going to give you some tips on taking better photos of your stuff.

Here's your Mandalinkian or whatever it's called. It looks about ten million times better, huh?

Well, here's how to do it . . .

101

Tip #1: BEWARE OF THE DARK SIDE!

You don't need a fancy camera or special lens or super-bright lights . . . you just need to . . .

GO OUTSIDE! Your pictures will instantly be a lot better if you just take them outside. During the DAY, obviously! The best thing you can do is to go out on a bright day, but find a place in the shade . . .

But make sure it's not a place that's got some shade AND some sun: that's distracting!

The one below was taken just a few inches away . . . where the sun wasn't hitting it directly . . .

Tip #2: FOCUS

See how the picture above is kinda blurry? I got too close!

If your camera has a "macro" or "flower" setting, use it!

If not, stay back and then zoom in using an app or online photo fixer. (There are plenty of free ones.)

Tip #3: SET UP A BACKDROP!

Don't be scared by the word "backdrop" . . . I just mean a blank piece of paper. This will help your origami stand out and also it will mean I don't have to see any more pictures of an origami dude standing on a wrinkly blanket.

Colored paper like construction paper works great.

Just put it down in a good place (tip #1) then put the origami down in the middle of it, then take your picture using tip #2.

This is all about getting rid of distractions so people get a good look at your origami and not my mom's sh'nasty old tablecloth! Here's me taking a picture of me taking a picture of that monkey pet of Jabba's.

It turned out pretty good . . .

Tip #4: CHOOSE BACKDROP COLOR WISELY

If you spend $1 to get a pack of different colored construction paper,
you'll be able to pick the color that's right for each puppet . . .

Darth Maul kind of blends into the black one and you can't even see
his horns on the white one. So pick a completely different color for him.

Now you can really see him!

You know what else would be cool?
If you used a computer to make a
really awesome backdrop.

Then you could just drop the
origami on there and TA-DA!

I guess I must be the nicest girl in
the whole school, because I made
two for you. I downloaded the *Star
Wars* logo at starwars.com.

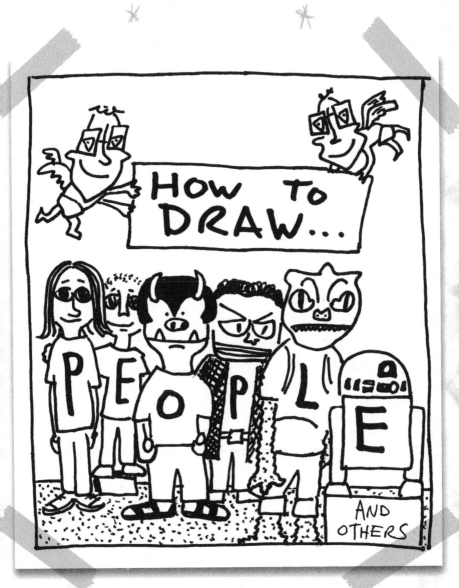

HOW TO DRAW
SHIRTS AND PANTS
BY KELLEN

IT MIGHT SEEM LIKE PEOPLE ARE HARD TO DRAW ...
BECAUSE THEY <u>ARE</u> HARD TO DRAW. BUT IT ISN'T
IMPOSSIBLE IF YOU TAKE IT ONE PIECE AT A TIME.
STARTING WITH ... A SHIRT, WHICH <u>IS</u> EASY.

IT'S JUST TWO TRIANGLES
STUCK ON THE SIDES OF A
RECTANGLE ...

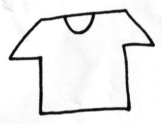

WITH A "U" IN
THE MIDDLE FOR THE
NECK HOLE.

MAKE THE TRIANGLES
A BIT CURVY, AND
DON'T DRAW ALL
THE LINES.

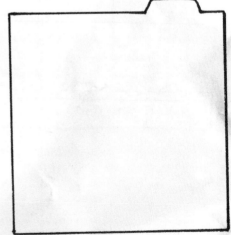

PRACTICE HERE UNTIL YOU HAVE
MASTERED THE SHIRT.

NOW ADD SOME PANTS...

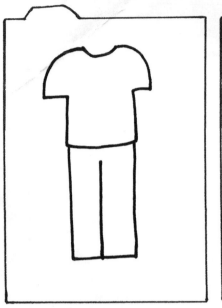

THEY'RE JUST A RECTANGLE WITH A LINE DOWN THE MIDDLE OR AN UPSIDE-DOWN "V"... AND SHORTS ARE JUST <u>SHORT</u> PANTS!

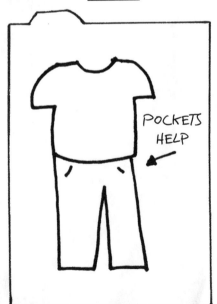

POCKETS HELP

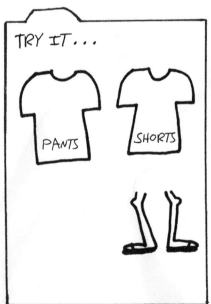

TRY IT...

PANTS

SHORTS

PRACTICE HERE UNTIL YOU HAVE MASTERED
DRAWING SHIRTS AND PANTS TOGETHER . . .

HOW TO DRAW SHOES

BY KELLEN

① P A N T S

② P A N T S

③ P A N T S

NOW ADD A FEW DETAILS...

JUST CHANGE ONE OR MORE OF THOSE THREE LINES...

TO GET LOTS OF DIFFERENT SHOE SHAPES!

 112

 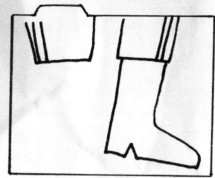

OR MAKE LINE 1 LONG ENOUGH TO MAKE LEIA'S AND HAN'S BOOTS.

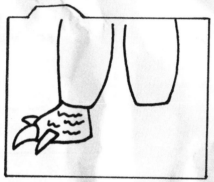 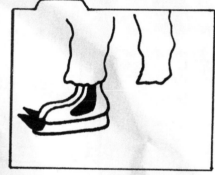

ADD SOME CLAWS FOR BOSSK.

DON'T FORGET BOBA'S TOE SPIKES!

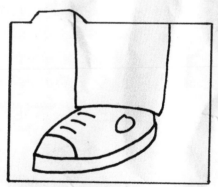 

TRY IT . . .

CURVE LINE 2 TO GIVE 3-D EFFECT.

BONUS TIP: DON'T FORGET STINK LINES FOR HARVEY'S SHOES!

HOW TO DRAW FAKE HANDS & ARMS

BY KELLEN

HANDS AND ARMS ARE HARD!!! IF YOU'RE NOT IN THE MOOD FOR A STRUGGLE, JUST TRY THESE FAKE ONES . . .

DRAW LINE DOWN BESIDE SHIRT . . .

DRAW MY OTHER ARM, PLEASE

ADD A CURVE FOR THE HAND AND EITHER A "U" OR A BACKWARD "J" FOR THE THUMB.

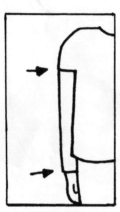

FOR LONG SLEEVES, JUST MOVE LINE DOWN.

A QUICK NOTE ABOUT WRITING ON T-SHIRTS:

STR8 LINES LOOK FLAT

CURVES LOOK BETTER

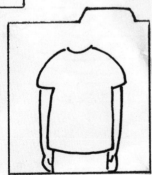

SHOW ME YOUR MASTERY OF
FAKE HANDS AND ARMS . . .

HOW TO DRAW HEADS

BY KELLEN

 OH, GREAT... HEADS ARE THE HARDEST PART TO DRAW!

NO... EASIEST THEY ARE...

IF A JEDI MIND TRICK YOU USE!

 SEE... ONCE YOU DRAW A BODY, ALMOST ANYTHING YOU DRAW ON TOP WILL LOOK LIKE A HEAD!

EVEN A BLOB WITH A SMILEY FACE OR A SCRIBBLE.

TRY IT OUT... DON'T WORRY ABOUT THE
FACES YET. A SMILEY WILL DO.

HOW TO DRAW EYES

BY KELLEN

FIRST OF ALL ... DON'T DRAW EYES LIKE THIS!

IT'S JUST GOING TO MAKE PEOPLE LOOK ALL FREAKY! UNLESS IT'S AHSOKA. →

EYES COME IN LOTS OF SHAPES, SO YOU REALLY NEED TO LOOK AT A PERSON BEFORE YOU DRAW THEIR EYES!

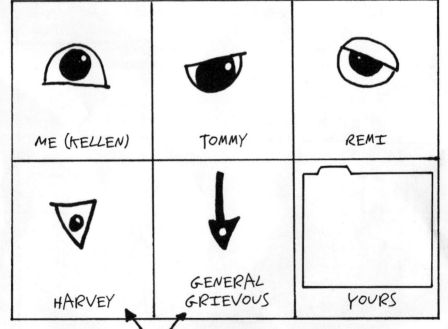

ME (KELLEN)	TOMMY	REMI
HARVEY	GENERAL GRIEVOUS	YOURS

ACTUALLY, SOME PEOPLE DO HAVE THE SAME SHAPE.

LOOK AT DIFFERENT PEOPLE AND TRY DRAWING JUST THEIR EYES . . .

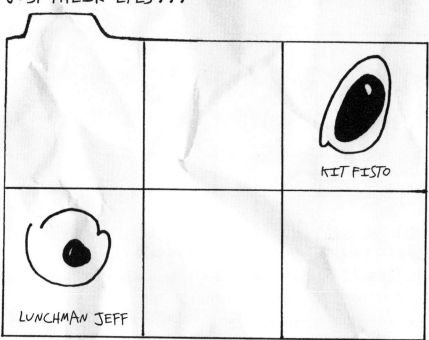

KIT FISTO

LUNCHMAN JEFF

NOW TRY DRAWING THOSE SAME EYES TINY!

BONUS POINTS IF YOU RECOGNIZE THESE EYES!

WHAT'S THE DIFFERENCE BETWEEN THESE TWO PICTURES OF DWIGHT?

THE ONE ON THE RIGHT HAS "EYESHINE"! EYESHINE IS ALWAYS A GOOD IDEA... BUT UNLESS YOU HAVE A WHITE PEN HANDY, YOU HAVE TO PLAN AHEAD!

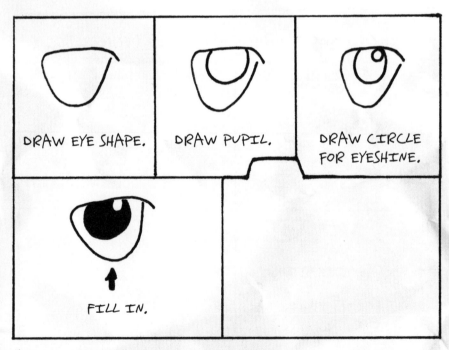

DRAW EYE SHAPE.

DRAW PUPIL.

DRAW CIRCLE FOR EYESHINE.

FILL IN.

A WORD ABOUT GLASSES...
THEY CAN BE HARD!!!

I LIKE TO DRAW THE GLASSES FIRST AND THEN ADD THE EYES. HERE'S HOW TO DRAW HARVEY'S EYES AND GLASSES.

TRY SOME...

I DO NOT HAVE SQUARE GLASSES! WHY DO YOU ALWAYS DRAW ME WITH SQUARE GLASSES? NOBODY HAS SQUARE GLASSES! AND MY EYES ARE NOT TRIANGLES, EITHER!!!!!!

HOW TO DRAW FACES

BY KELLEN

ONCE YOU CAN
DRAW EYES...

...A FACE IS JUST
PUTTING A NOSE IN
BETWEEN AND A LINE
UNDERNEATH FOR A
MOUTH.
(I LIKE TO ADD AN
EXTRA LINE UNDER
THE MOUTH LINE.)

THEN ADD SOME HAIR.
AND DRAW A SINGLE
LINE THAT STARTS
WITH ONE EAR,
GOES AROUND THE
FACE, AND ENDS
WITH THE OTHER EAR.

SARA

TOMMY

LUNCHMAN JEFF

TRY THESE FACES . . .

123

DRAW YOUR FAVORITE STAR WARS GOOD GUY.

DRAW YOUR FAVORITE STAR WARS BAD GUY.

DRAW YOURSELF AND YOUR BEST FRIEND . . .

HOW TO
DRAW HANDS
BY KELLEN

HANDS ARE THE HARDEST THING IN THE <u>UNIVERSE</u> TO DRAW! I'M NOT CLAIMING TO BE ANY GOOD AT IT. (SO DON'T START, HARVEY!!!) BUT HERE ARE MY HAND-DRAWING SURVIVAL TIPS!

I TOOK A PICTURE OF TOMMY'S HAND, THEN LOADED IT UP ON MY COMPUTER. THEN I DREW A LINE AROUND IT. HERE'S WHAT I FOUND OUT...

THE FINGERS ARE...

THERE'S A SPACE HERE ABOVE THE THUMB BEFORE YOU GET TO THE FINGERS...

THE THUMB STICKS OUT AT AN ANGLE...

THIS "V" LINE COMES DOWN FARTHER THAN THE OTHER "V" LINES.

AND THERE'S A LONG SPACE UNDER THE LITTLE FINGER BEFORE THE HAND CURVES INTO THE WRIST...

NOW LET'S SEE IF WE CAN USE ALL THAT INFO TO DRAW A HAND.

THE THUMB STICKS OUT AT AN ANGLE.

DRAW ALONG HERE . . .

THERE'S A SPACE ABOVE THE THUMB.

THE FINGERS ARE MEDIUM, BIG, MEDIUM . . . (REMEMBER, THIS "v" COMES DOWN FARTHER) . . . AND LITTLE.

THEN THERE'S A SPACE UNDER THE LITTLE FINGER. THEN THE HAND CURVES INTO THE WRIST.

127

DRAWING A CLOSED HAND IS A BIT EASIER.

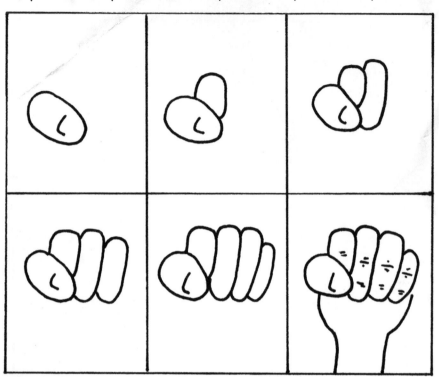

TRY A RIGHT HAND . . .

AND A LEFT . . .

THE BEST THING TO DO IS TO AVOID DRAWING HANDS IN THE FIRST PLACE! HAVE YOUR DOODLE PERSON HOLD A:

JUST DRAW A BOX AND LEAVE A HOLE FOR THE THUMB!

HOLE FOR THUMB

BUT DON'T DO THIS!

YOU'RE NOT FOOLING ANYBODY!
PLUS, IT LOOKS LIKE THIS DUDE IS PEEING!

FRAMES ARE THE BEST WAY EVER TO AVOID DRAWING HANDS! JUST CUT PEOPLE OFF ABOVE THE HANDS AND YOU'RE DONE! PLUS, FRAMES MAKE YOUR DOODLES LOOK LIKE ART.

OH YEAH, FRAMES WORK GREAT ON MOUTHS, TOO!

... AND THEN DRAW ANOTHER LINE NEXT TO IT ...
AND ADD A HAND.

DRAW OUTSIDES OF LEGS.

THEN INSIDES.

THEN SHOES!

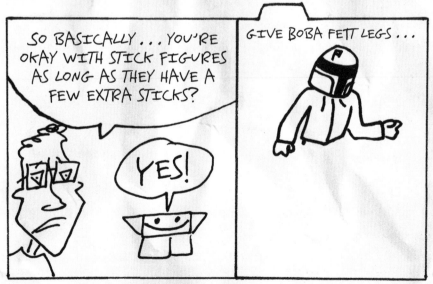

NOW THAT YOU'VE MASTERED PEOPLE,
IT'S TIME FOR . . .

HOW TO BLOW YOUR NOSE!

THIS BOOKMARK COULD SAVE YOUR LIFE!!!!!!!!!!!!

Mr. Good Clean Fun and Soapy here to remind you of our five easy LIFE-SAVING steps for blowing your nose!

1) Wash hands before dispensing tissue from box.
2) Dispense the amount of tissues you need — DON'T BE WASTEFUL!!!
3) Completely cover nostrils and blow firmly, but politely.
4) After using your tissue, please dispose of it in a proper receptacle.
5) Wash hands — AGAIN — after using the tissue.

Follow these steps for fewer sick days and more GOOD CLEAN FUN Days!

Photocopy this page and cut out your own bookmark.

133

HOW TO TALK LIKE YODA

BY HARVEY

okay ... now I'm going to add something USEFUL to this case file! I think the one thing we can all agree on is that I do the best Yoda impression ← around here!

The important thing is to know what order to put the words in.

It is NOT just saying them backward! That's a common mistake, but WRONG!

> ## I talk like Yoda!

> ## Yoda like talk I!

See? That stinks! And you can't fix it just by adding "do" to the end ... like SOME people do.

> ## Yoda like talk I do!

Instead, you need to move the subject to the end...

> ① **Talk like Yoda**

Now is the time to add "do" or another verb to help the sentence make sense...

> **Talk like Yoda I do!**

Now add a "hmmm" or a "yes?"...

> **Talk like Yoda I do, yes?**

Sometimes it's better to move the subject AND the verb to the end...

> **Harvey is the greatest!**

> **The greatest Harvey is!**

Try these:
The dark side is powerful.
You must buy Cheetos for everyone.
fools rush in.
Do you judge me by my size?

NOSE PICKER

135

TRENCH RUN
THE 56¢ STAR WARS GAME
BY MIKE AND KELLEN

YOU WILL NEED:

PLUS TWO PLAYERS, A TABLE, AND TWO OR MORE BOOKS!

FIRST... LEARN TO FIRE A PHOTON PENNY!

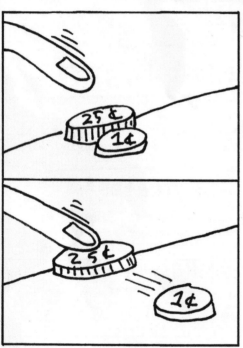

PLACE PENNY SO IT TOUCHES EDGE OF QUARTER.

THEN...

STRIKE QUARTER WITH ONE FINGER!

THE PENNY SHOOTS OFF!

(GEORGE WASHINGTON, REBEL LEADER)

136

RULES:

- TAKE TURNS FIRING PHOTON PENNIES.
- KNOCK NICKEL COMPLETELY CLEAR OF QUARTER TO GET POINT.
- TOUCH BOOKS OR GO OFF TABLE AND YOU LOSE A TURN!
- TOO EASY? ADD MORE BOOKS! SLIDE BOOKS CLOSER TOGETHER! STACK EXTRA QUARTER ON TARGET!
- USE THE FORCE!

HOW TO MAKE A LIP BALM ROCKET

BY DWIGHT AND KELLEN

OPEN UP A TUBE OF LIP STUFF AND TURN THE KNOB TO CRANK THE LIP BALM ALL THE WAY OUT...

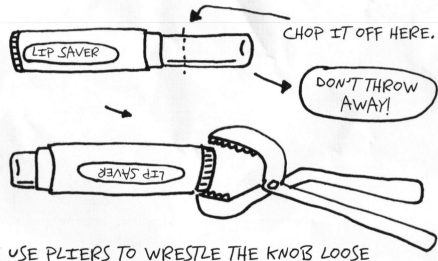

CHOP IT OFF HERE.

DON'T THROW AWAY!

USE PLIERS TO WRESTLE THE KNOB LOOSE AT THE BOTTOM. (DO NOT USE A KNIFE!)

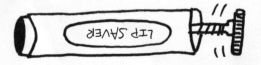

HOPEFULLY, KNOB WILL COME LOOSE BUT WILL STILL BE CONNECTED TO SOMETHING INSIDE THE TUBE. IF NOT, IT CAN PROBABLY BE SCREWED BACK IN.

NOTE: DWIGHT'S METHOD OF BEATING ON THE TUBE WITH A VOLUME OF THE ENCYCLOPEDIA IS <u>NOT</u> RECOMMENDED! IT TAKES <u>FOREVER</u>!

NOW USE THE ACTUAL BALM STUFF TO GREASE THE MOUTH OF THE TUBE A LITTLE BIT. YOU MAY NEED TO APPLY MORE OR WIPE SOME OFF, DEPENDING ON HOW THINGS GO...

SMEAR

NOW PUT ON THE CAP...

LIP SAVER

AIM UP (AND AWAY FROM YOUR FACE, DUH!)

SWING YOUR HAND AND HIT THE KNOB HARD...

WHEN THE PLUNGER GOES IN... THE CAP SHOULD POP OFF AND GO A LONG WAY!

LIP SAVER

SHOOT YOUR EYE OUT YOU MUST NOT!

HOW DWIGHT FAKE-CRACKS HIS KNUCKLES
BY TOMMY

At last I have solved the mystery of how Dwight drives everyone crazy by fake-cracking his knuckles. Now I can do it, too! Here's how:

1. Put the index finger of your left hand between the index and middle fingers of your right hand.

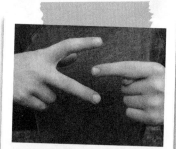

2. It should look like this. The tip of your index finger is pushing down on the web between the other two fingers.

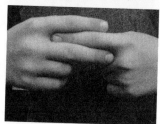

3. Now place all three fingers firmly against your chin. You must create an airtight seal so that a little pocket of air is formed above your left index finger.

4. Now bend your left index finger down quickly! When it pops loose from the other fingers, the air bubble should pop, too, making a loud CRACK!

It takes a lot of practice, but soon you will be able to annoy a whole roomful of people!!! Good luck, and use your powers wisely!

HOW TO MAKE ERASER PRINTS

BY MURKY AND KELLEN

OKAY, YOU ARE GOING TO NEED ONE OF THOSE BIG ERASERS. SOME OF THEM ARE PINK. IT DOESN'T MATTER WHAT COLOR IT IS. I'M JUST SAYING THAT A LOT OF THEM ARE PINK.

YOU ALSO NEED A COUPLE OF DECENT MAGIC MARKERS BUT NOT SHARPIES. SHARPIES ARE STOOKY BUT NOT FOR THIS. YOU JUST NEED REGULAR DECENT MAGIC MARKERS FOR THIS.

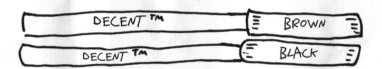

SO DRAW A BUNCH OF HAIR ON THE FLAT PART OF THE ERASER. IT'S JUST A LOT OF LITTLE LINES SO DON'T WASTE A WHOLE LOT OF TIME. IF YOU DO, THE INK WILL DRY AND YOU'LL BE LIKE "HUH?"

AS SOON AS YOU FINISH DRAWING, FLIP IT OVER ON A PIECE OF PAPER AND SMOOSH IT DOWN MEGA HARD, THEN LIFT IT UP CAREFULLY SO YOU DON'T SMEAR IT.

141

OKAY, NOW YOU SHOULD HAVE A PRINT LIKE THIS. IF YOU SMUDGE IT, DON'T WORRY. CHEWIE WON'T MIND.

NOW USE THE BLACK MARKER TO DRAW CHEWIE'S FACE ON THE ERASER.

AND DRAW THE BANDOLIER BACKWARDS.

YOU'RE MAKING A PRINT AND PRINTED STUFF COMES OUT BACKWARDS, SO DRAW IT BACKWARDS NOW OR IT WILL BE BACKWARDS LATER. AND DON'T WASTE TIME. DO IT QUICK.

NOW FLIP IT OVER ON TOP OF THE CHEWIE HAIR PRINT AND SMOOSH AGAIN.

YOU SHOULD GET SOMETHING LIKE THIS. IF NOT, JUST TRY AGAIN. THE ERASER WILL BE DRY IN TWO SECONDS.

TO MAKE CHEWIE'S ARMS

DRAW SOME HAIR ON THE SIDE OF THE ERASER...

THEN BEND IT... POSITION IT... <u>SMOOSH</u> IT!

THEN GIVE HIM SOME LEGS.

YOU CAN MAKE LOTS OF STAR WARS PEOPLE... EVEN ART2-D2!

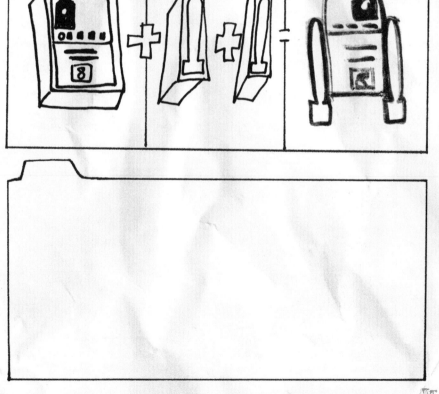

ACTION FIGURE AND SPACESHIP PRINTS

BY AMY

Okay, so this is not really doodling. You may end up with a big inky mess. Or you may end up with something good enough to hang in a museum. It's all a bit random, so just have fun!

You will need:

• Silly Putty (You can try stuff like modeling clay, but Silly Putty works great! I used three eggs' worth on the *Millennium Falcon*.)

• Stamp pad (You can also try using Magic Markers.)

• *Star Wars* toys! (If you are careful, they should be okay, but don't try this with a rare antique or something. And you'll see that some toys work better than others . . .)

1. Flatten Silly Putty into a blob the same size as the toy . . .

2. Then push the toy facedown into the Silly Putty . . .

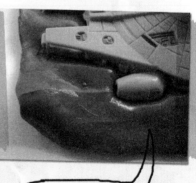

3. Carefully peel the putty off the toy . . . You now have a mold of the toy!

4. Working quickly, dab your finger on the ink pad, then dab it on the putty. Continue until the entire surface is good and inky! *Don't* try to fill in all the little nooks and crannies . . . those are what make the print!

5. Now flip the putty over so it is ink side down on the paper . . . and smoosh it all down really, really good with your fingers . . .

6. Now peel back the putty to reveal your print!!!

Don't worry if it's not perfect . . . it's not supposed to be!

Tips:

- Just knead the putty a bit and you'll be ready to use it again!
- Which is good, because sometimes it takes three or four tries to get a good one.
- Try scanning or photographing your prints and adjusting the colors, contrast, and size.
- You can use two toys to make one print. For the Chewie print below, I molded a section of the Falcon, then I molded Chewie on top of that.
- Experimenting is key! Some figures, like Jabba, work great; some, like Salacious Crumb, don't (Crumb's nose is too pointy!).

PRACTICE AND PATIENCE THE KEY ARE, PADAWAN... REGULAR PAPER YOU MAY USE UNTIL READY TO MAKE PRINT BELOW YOU ARE...

Make a print here . . .

PENCIL PODRACING
BY MIKE

Okay, remember when Mr. Snider taught us how to play that old Pencil Wars game where X-wings and TIE fighters battle around the Death Star? Well, that game is stooky, but I actually like Pencil Podracing even better. We made it up, and here are the rules . . .

Just like with the other game, you move your ship/podracer with pencil flicks . . .

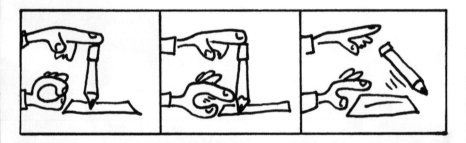

Press down on the eraser end of the pencil with your left index finger so that the tip is right in front of your podracer. Then flick the pencil near the bottom with your right index finger. If you do it right, it should make a mark on the paper . . . Wherever the mark goes, that's where your podracer goes! So redraw the podracer at the end of the mark.

In this game you race around an obstacle course. (Making the obstacle courses is almost as much fun as playing!) You have to flick the pencil so that you go as far as possible . . . but you also have to avoid all the obstacles!

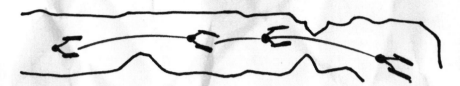

If you don't hit anything, you redraw your podracer at the end of the mark, and then the next person goes.

If you hit a wall, you redraw your podracer at the spot where you hit the wall, and your turn is over.

If you hit an obstacle with a label (such as -1 or -2), then your turn is over, and you also miss future turns . . .

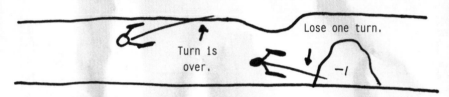

If you hit another podracer, they lose a turn! So playing like Sebulba can really pay off!

You may also hit something that gives you an extra turn (+1) or maybe a bunch of extra turns. But don't put in too many of these or the game gets dumb.

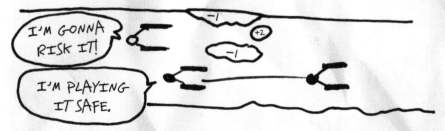

A well-designed course tempts the players into taking Anakin-level risks to get any rewards!

Beginner podracing course

Draw your own . . .

151

Expert podracing course

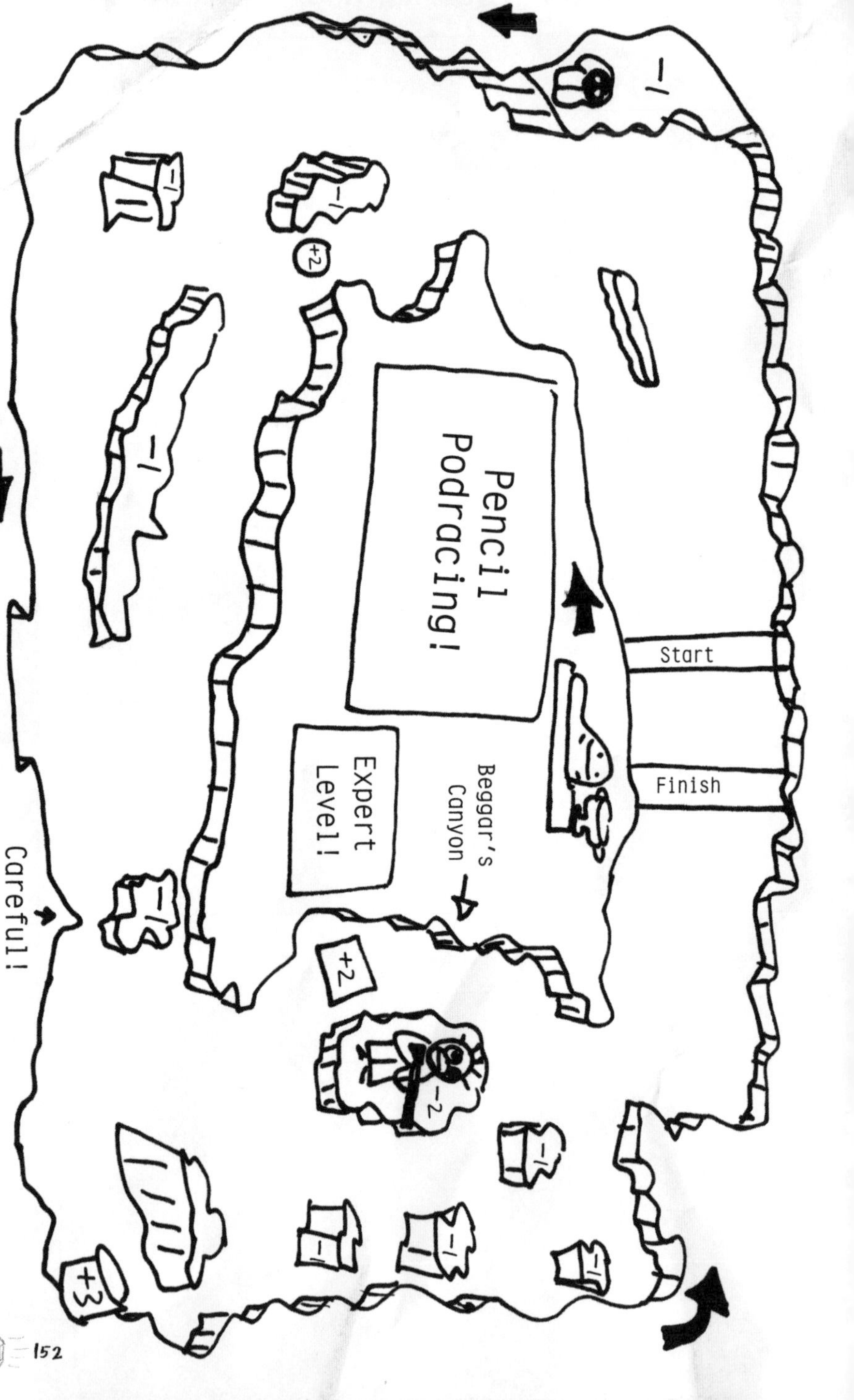

Pencil Podracing!

Expert Level!

Beggar's Canyon

Start

Finish

Careful!

+2

-1

-1

-1

-1

-1

-1

-1

-1

-2

+2

+3

!

152

Draw your own . . .

153

HOW TO MAKE YOUR OWN ORIGAMI YODA T-SHIRT

BY KELLEN

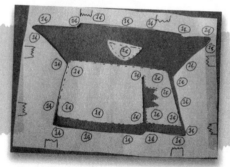

<u>WARNING</u>: THIS PROJECT IS A GREAT WAY TO MAKE YOUR MOM MAD! I KNOW <u>THAT FOR A FACT</u>! SO USE SOME COMMON SENSE . . . MAKE IT OUTSIDE, USE AN OLD SHIRT, BE CAREFUL WITH THE SPRAY PAINT, ETC. . . .

YOU WILL NEED:
- WHITE T-SHIRT
- GREEN SPRAY PAINT
- SCISSORS
- TAPE
- BLACK SHARPIE
- SCRAP PAPER
- FLAT SPOT OUTSIDE
- A BUNCH OF PENNIES (AND MAYBE A DIME)

1. CUT OUT STENCIL PAGE AND CUT OUT STENCIL ON SOLID BLACK OUTLINE.

2. CUT OUT THE INSIDE PIECES OF THE STENCIL.

3. NOW LAY THE SHIRT ON SOMETHING FLAT THAT YOU WON'T GET IN TROUBLE IF YOU GET PAINT ON IT. I USED THE LID OF A PLASTIC TUB . . .

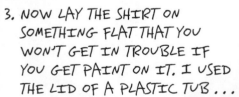

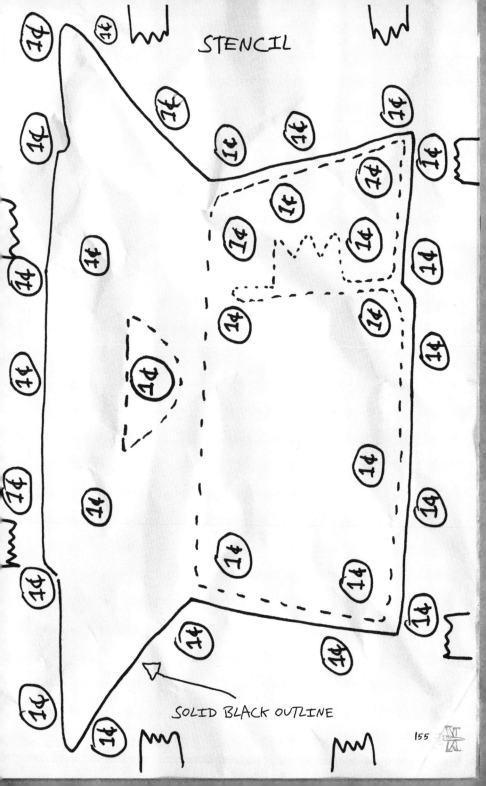

STENCIL

SOLID BLACK OUTLINE

155

IF YOU'RE NOT GOING TO MAKE A T-SHIRT, YOU MAY AS WELL DOODLE HERE. BUT IF YOU ARE GOING TO, THEN DON'T DOODLE HERE, BECAUSE YOU'LL HAVE TO CUT IT UP!

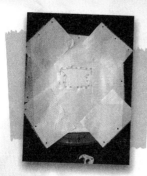

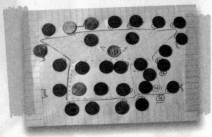

4. LAY STENCIL IN THE CENTER OF THE T-SHIRT (TWO OR THREE INCHES BELOW THE NECK HOLE). TAPE SCRAP PAPER TO THE EDGES OF THE STENCIL AND ALL AROUND. COVER AS MUCH OF THE SHIRT AS POSSIBLE.

5. NOW USE THE PENNIES TO ANCHOR THE STENCIL IN PLACE, LEAVING T-SHIRT EXPOSED. YOU MAY NEED TO USE A DIME ON THE MOUTH, IF IT'S TOO SMALL. AND ADD TWO EXTRA PENNIES TO CREATE THE EYES!!!!

6. START SPRAYING! DON'T GET TOO CLOSE . . . IF YOU BLAST THE STENCIL, THE PAINT WILL GET UNDERNEATH IT!

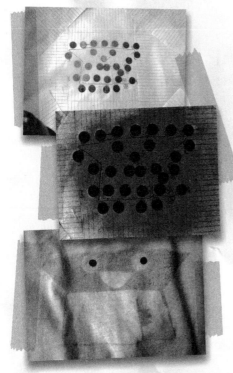

7. GIVE IT A FEW MINUTES TO DRY. THEN CAREFULLY PEEL EVERYTHING OFF AND YOU SHOULD SEE ORIGAMI YODA UNDERNEATH!

8. ADD EYES WITH A SHARPIE AND WEAR YOUR SHIRT WITH PRIDE!!!!!!! (LOOKS BETTER IN COLOR.)

Great, what am I supposed to do with a bunch of green pennies?

Harvey's Comment

157

THE END IS THE BEGINNING

BY TOMMY

Well, I have to admit I was a little disappointed at first. Not really with the case file but with my doodling and stuff.

My AT-AT looks like Luke has already blown it up. My lip balm rocket hit my brother in the head, and I got in huge trouble. My T-shirt turned out okay, but I wish I had used green paint, because everybody who sees it asks me, "Uh, why is Yoda red? Is it, like, Darth Yoda or something?" And also, yes, I managed to make my mom mad by getting paint on the driveway.

AT-AT
BY TOMMY →

But my doodling is the worst! All my pictures of people look like I'm trying to insult them.

About the only thing I got right was a perfect picture of an Ugnaught. Unfortunately, I was TRYING to draw Sara when I made it! And as far as drawing hands . . . forget it!

So I felt like a total loser . . . until Kellen made me show him and Dwight and Sara what I had done.

"This picture of me doesn't look like an Ugnaught!" said Sara. "It's sweet! Can I keep it? And your smileys are awesome!"

"Yeah, dude, this is stooky stuff," Kellen said. "I'm glad they don't look exactly like the ones in the case file. You've got your own style! And the case file wasn't supposed to turn you into a master. It was just supposed to get you started."

"Yes! Beyond the case file you must go," said Origami Yoda. "Any piece of scrap paper become art it can. Like this one . . . Doodle all over it you must . . ."

Harvey Cunningham II
Ms. Bauer
Third Period

Biography Unit
Assignment 3
Autobiography

I was born in Roanoke but have always lived here.

My parents realized that I was gifted when I was four months old.

My special areas of expertise include math, reading, grammar, spelling, U.S. history, American geography, world history, world geography, movies, science fiction movies, science, biology, entomology (the study of arachnids and insects), advanced chemistry, software development and programming, and, of course, origami.

My origami creations have been featured in the newspaper and have received as many as thirty-seven likes on photowallrus.com.

Currently a seventh grader, I am already taking several college-level web classes and performing exceptionally well in them.

In the future, I think my greatest difficulty will be in deciding which one of my many talents I should pursue as a career.

Then one day I can write another autobiography, which will be a bestseller and will give me a chance to share my knowledge and ideas with the world.

"An important journey you have begun. Complete is your training, but forever will your skills improve," said Origami Yoda. "Cut off your Padawan braid you may."

"Uh . . . I don't have a Padawan braid," I said. "You made me shave my head, remember?"

"Right, yeah, oh . . . ," said Origami Yoda. "Anyway . . ."

"Beep blee-beep," said Kellen, and I thought he had gone crazy, until I realized he was holding Art2 and C-3PO.

"Well done, sir!" said C-3PO. "Might I suggest that the next things you make are some legs for me? It's really quite dreadful without them!"

"Maybe we should tape you onto the back of the Fortune Wookiee," said Sara. "That way you can reenact the last half of *The Empire Strikes Back*!"

"Oh no!" yelled C-3PO/Kellen. "Not that flea-bitten fur ball again! Legs would be quite preferable!"

"But there weren't any instructions!" I said.

"Beep whistle!" went Art2.

"Okay, okay," I said, "I'll figure it out myself!"

"Yes!" said Origami Yoda. "Doodling, folding, and experimenting you must continue. Mistakes will you make, but better and more powerful you will become. That is the way of the Jedi Doodler . . . Finished you may be, but only begun you have."

Harvey's Comment

Well, that was annoying. By the way, has anybody seen my homework for Ms. Bauer's class? I have to turn it in in five minutes!

Tommy's Comment: No comment.

163

TOMMY AND KELLEN'S BIBLIOGRAPHY

BY TOMMY AND KELLEN

Here are some of the books we used for inspiration, reference, and learning to draw/fold in the first place:

More *Star Wars* Stuff to Make:
Star Wars Origami (Chris Alexander)
The Star Wars Craft Book (Bonnie Burton)
Star Wars Folded Flyers (Ben Harper & *Klutz*)

How to Draw:
Ed Emberly's Drawing Book: Make a World, Ed Emberly's Big Green Book, and a bunch more (Ed Emberly)
Animation (Preston Blair)

How to Fold:
Any origami book you can get your hands on! (Robert Lang, John Montroll, Won Park, and many more!)

Reference:
The Illustrated Star Wars Universe (Ralph McQuarrie and Kevin Anderson)

Millennium Falcon: A 3-D Owner's Guide (Ryder Windham, Chris Trevas, Chris Reiff)
The Making of Star Wars (J. W. Rinzler)
Star Wars: Head to Head (Pablo Hidalgo)
Star Wars: The Visual Dictionary (DK)
Star Wars: The Clone Wars Visual Guide (DK)
Star Wars: Character Encylopedia (DK)
Star Wars: The Clone Wars Character Encyclopedia (DK)

Stooky:
Star Wars: A Galactic Pop-Up Adventure and *Star Wars: A Pop-Up Guide to the Galaxy* (Matthew Reinhart)

Healthy:
Booger-Free You, Booger-Free Me! (Brian "Mr. Good Clean Fun" Compton)

Dwight says this is the book that got him started in the first place: *Curious George Rides a Bike* (H. A. Rey). I know it doesn't sound like an origami book, but it is, sorta!

And, even though they are movies and TV shows and not books: *The Phantom Menace, Attack of the Clones, THE CLONE WARS!!!!* (the television series), *Revenge of the Sith, A New Hope, The Empire Strikes Back,* and *Return of the Jedi*

ABOUT THE AUTHOR

Tom Angleberger is the author of the *New York Times* bestselling Origami Yoda series, which includes *The Strange Case of Origami Yoda*, *Darth Paper Strikes Back*, and *The Secret of the Fortune Wookiee*. He is also the author of *Fake Mustache* and *Horton Halfpott*, an Edgar Award nominee. Visit him online at www.origamiyoda.com. Tom lives in the Appalachian Mountains of Virginia with his wife, author-illustrator Cece Bell, who taught him how to draw dogs.

This book was designed by Melissa J. Arnst and art directed by Chad W. Beckerman. Twenty fonts were used to bring this book to life, including the brand new font ANGLEBERGER! The main text is set in 10-point Lucida Sans Typewriter. The display typeface is ERASER. Tommy's comments are set in Kienan, and Harvey's comments are set in Good Dog. The hand lettering on the cover was done by Jason Rosenstock.

KEEP READING BOOKS BY BESTSELLING AUTHOR TOM ANGLEBERGER!

Author of the bestselling **ORIGAMI YODA** series

For the **FIRST-CLASS MAN-ABOUT-TOWN** *look*

FAKE MUSTACHE

WARNING: WEAR WITH CARE

HOW JODIE O'RODEO AND HER WONDER HORSE (AND SOME NERDY KID) SAVED THE U.S. PRESIDENTIAL ELECTION FROM A MAD GENIUS CRIMINAL MASTERMIND

TOM ANGLEBERGER